11-07 BK. Bud. Aug.

P9-CEP-814

HQ
759.92
.A55
2000

Stepmothers and Stepdaughters

Relationships of Chance, Friendships for a Lifetime

KAREN L. ANNARINO

with Jean M. Blomquist

SOUTHEASTERN COMMUNITY
COLLEGE LIBRARY
WHITEVILLE, NC 28472

WILDCAT CANYON PRESS
A Division of Circulus Publishing Group, Inc.
Berkeley, California

Stepmothers and Stepdaughters: Relationships of Chance, Friendships for a Lifetime

Copyright © 2000 by Karen Annarino and Jean M. Blomquist
Cover Photo by Jeff Dunas/The Image Bank

All Rights Reserved under International and Pan-American Copyright
Conventions. Published in the United States by Wildcat Canyon Press, a division of Circulus Publishing Group, Inc. No part of this book may be reproduced in whole or in part without written permission from the publisher,
except by a reviewer who may quote brief passages in a review; nor may any
part of this book be reproduced, stored in a retrieval system, or transmitted in
any form or by any means electronic, mechanical, photocopying, recording, or
other, without written permission from the publisher.

Publisher: Tamara Traeder
Editorial Director: Roy M. Carlisle
Marketing Director: Carol Brown
Managing Editor: Leyza Yardley
Production Coordinator: Larissa Berry
Copyeditor: Holly Taines White
Cover Design: Mary Beth Salmon
Interior Design and Typesetting: Margaret Copeland/Terragraphics
Typographic Specifications: Text in Caslon Regular 11.5/15,
   headings in Caslon Bold.

Printed in Canada

Cataloging-in-Publication Data
Annarino,Karen,1964-
    Stepmothers & stepdaughters : relationships of chance, friendships for a
    lifetime /Karen Annarino with Jean M. Blomquist.
        p.cm.
    Includes bibliographical references.
    ISBN 1-885171-46-3 (alk.paper)
    1.Stepmothers. 2. Stepdaughters. I.Title: Stepmothers and
stepdaughters. II. Blomquist, Jean M. III. Title.

HQ759.92 .A55 2000
306.874—dc21

Distributed to the trade by Publishers Group West
10 9 8 7 6 5 4 3 2 1   04 03 02 01 00

Contents

Acknowledgments ❀ iv
Preface ❀ vi
Introduction ❀ 1

DISCOVERY—Learning as We Go ❀ 11
Getting to Know You . . . and You . . . and You, Beginning Our Lives Together, Ditching the Wicked Stepmother

DEEPENING—Facing the Challenges of Life Together ❀ 45
Changing, Changing, Everything's Changing, Lowering Expectations/Holding on to Hope, Encountering Ourselves and Others Anew, Bridging Family Gaps

DARING—Creating New Ways of Being Family ❀ 79
Discovering Who We Are, Birthing a New Family, Growing Together: Moms, Stepmoms, and Stepdaughters, Being There for Those We Love

DELIGHT—Gathering the Gifts of Life Together ❀ 135
Letting Go and Choosing Love, Embracing Mysteries of Life, Celebrating Our Love

CONCLUSION ❀ 157

SHARING OUR WISDOM—Advice to Steps and Soon-to-Be Steps ❀ 163
Stepmothers Speak to Stepmothers, Stepdaughters Speak to Stepdaughters

Notes ❀ 169

About the Author ❀ 170

About the Press ❀ 171

Acknowledgments

I am deeply grateful for the stepmothers and stepdaughters that have graciously allowed me into their lives over the last several months. The insight and candor of their intimate stories offered me a better understanding of a relationship that has been a part of my life for the past several years.

To Wildcat Canyon Press for believing there was a goal worth working towards. Tamara Traeder, my publisher, for being willing to take the risk on a first book. Roy M. Carlisle, my editor: You have been invaluable in this first phase of my writing career. Your insight and confidence has guided me through the best and the most difficult of times. I appreciate you very much.

Carol Brown, Leia Carlton, Nenelle Bunnin, and Leyza Yardley: For the hard work and coordination you have collectively endured. I value all of your dedication, e-mails, and words of encouragement along the way.

Sherry Powell: I am so touched by your immediate support. Thank you for sharing your thoughts and your family with me. Those e-mails remain very special to me.

Holly Taines White: For your fearless copyediting and thoughtful queries at a crucial stage in life of the project.

To Jean Blomquist: You are an angel. I can't express enough, my gratitude for sharing with me your expertise and guidance.

To Marisa Catlin: From the book fair to many proposals and transcriptions later . . . You are a valued friend without whom none of this would be possible. I am grateful.

To Jamie: For your invaluable friendship during this journey.

To Susan M. Taylor: For your months of insight that allowed me to see the way.

And to friends Rob Mendelow, Danny Pelchat, J.P. Gay, Roger Parent, Francois Perron, Anne Plomondon, Bill Ewart, Carolina Ewart, Rhonda Jones, Jaboli Hicks, Athena Ubach, Sean Kanan, Carla, Kristian and Xavier Orozco, Chris Dreyer, Erin Fleming, Elizabeth Amini, and Dominique Cady, thank you for being there.

I would like to thank and acknowledge every woman that participated and allowed me into her lives. This book hopefully validates and offers an outlet for their voice. Without them there would be no book to share.

Preface

The inspiration to write this book began many years ago, though I wasn't aware of it at the time. I was just seven years old when I met my future stepmother, Linda. A wonderfully bright and vivacious woman, she has made a profound and lasting impression on my life. As I look back at my childhood ideals of womanhood and adulthood, I realize that Linda brought traditions and invaluable experiences that have helped mold me into the person I am today.

Linda, however, is not the only woman who has touched my life in very important ways. I am fortunate in having had two female role models in my life—Linda and my mother, Ann. I cannot stress enough that the successful relationship I've had with my stepmother in large part grew out of the strength and insight of my courageous mother. From each of these influential yet distinctly different women, I have received many precious gifts, both significant and subtle.

Looking at my mother and my stepmother as mentors, I see now that my combined family situation offered me the opportunity to learn and prosper from two feminine points of view, a veritable galaxy of thoughts, ideals, and impressions. My mother and stepmother each supported me and chose to make me a priority in their lives. They did not let their personal feelings—about divorce, remarriage, ex-wives, and ex-husbands—negate what was most important to them—that I grow up in a healthy, positive, loving environment. I received so much love from my parents and stepparents that I was able to have a unique and nurturing childhood. As I've grown older, I've come to value my upbringing more and more.

As a child and teenager, however, I didn't always feel so positively about my experience. Living within the structure of a divorced family was difficult at times to understand, and, of course, was a choice I did not make. Kids don't like to be different, and my life was unlike that of most of my friends, who were with both of their parents at the dinner table and at family gatherings.

To say that I did not miss the life of the nuclear family would be far from true, but I never knew any other way. I longed for my family to get back together and fantasized that Mom, Dad, and I would someday all eat dinner together. I experienced feelings of sadness and abandonment. At times I felt alone, separated from my friends and classmates. But my parents have been divorced since I was two, and the truth is, although I've fantasized about it, I can't even imagine that cozy dinner scene actually happening.

Even as I daydreamed about another way of growing up, I was also aware of skills and capacities that were growing within me, precisely because of my situation. I gained the ability to be flexible. I learned to adjust to my parents' choices even though I was very rebellious at times. (Although rebellion was very tempting at times, I chose instead to go with the grain of the life my parents created.) I also acquired a certain intuition and insight that I otherwise would not have experienced at that age. I became more adultlike in my thinking and in my approach to my studies, friends, and future. I saw my parents for what they were—and were not—able to do.

Unlike many stepchildren, I did not resist the marriage of my father and my stepmother. Prior to their marriage, my relationship with Linda was one of friendship. She was never a peer, but a valued older friend. That friendship has continued and deepened considerably through the years. I have never called Linda "my mother," and we have been able to laugh off the negative "wicked stepmother" and "evil stepdaughter" stereotypes. The love and friendship we shared, and continue to share, clearly debunked those old myths.

My life with Linda was one of sharing—both practical and personal. Linda taught me how to prepare large holiday dinners, do needlepoint, and fold sheets to perfection. By example, Linda, a skilled housewife, showed me how to keep a family in order, raise a child, and regularly juggle a hundred or so extracurricular activities. She is also a writer—and a very good one at that.

Linda and I have gone through a lot over twenty-five years together, sharing life experiences ranging from births and marriages to breakups, illnesses, and deaths. She continues to be a trusted and dear confidante. Linda is also someone who gives me hope and courage. When I was twenty-five and survived a hit-and-run accident, Linda nursed me back to health. When doctors told me that I would never walk again, Linda proved them wrong. As my biggest fan, she cheered me on. When I lived at my father's after the accident, she changed my bandages, gave me showers, and pushed my wheelchair. When I felt hopeless, she gave me the strength to believe that one day I would put this difficult situation behind me. With Linda at my side, along with my loving mom and dad, I did just that, or more precisely, *we* did just that—together.

Very soon after I was able to walk, Linda was diagnosed with multiple sclerosis, a disease that I then knew very little about. Over the last several years, Linda's illness has progressed, taking over her body muscle by muscle, until she is now unable to walk or pick things up with her hands. My energetic, enthusiastic, and team-spirited stepmother now spends her days in a chair trying her best to keep her life normal. I help her get her scooter in and out of the car. I help her shower and organize things in her life so they run more smoothly. We still go out together and do our favorite things—shop, eat, and see movies.

Ironically, the roles have been reversed. I have wanted to tell her what she once told me, "One day this will all be behind you," but in her case, I know that each day, each moment, is the single most beautiful moment she has left.

Remembering that each and every moment now counts for Linda has helped me appreciate my life. As I look back on all the times I felt angry at my parents for the breakup of our family, or for pulling me in and out of schools so I had to change friends, or for having to say good-bye to someone I loved, I realize now that they always worked hard to maintain a stable home for me, a home where I would feel loved and cared for.

Along with my parents, Linda played a crucial role in creating that stable home for me. She will never take the place of my mother, but she has been an amazing addition to my life. We have seen each other through the best and worst of times, and we are still friends who deeply love each other. No matter what happens in my father and Linda's life together, I know that I will always have her in mine. Chance brought us together, but friendship and love keep us together—and for that I am deeply grateful.

It is because of my relationship with Linda that I am writing this book. For much too long the negative stereotypes of the "wicked stepmother" and "evil stepdaughter" have prevailed. Though, of course, not all step relationships are stellar, many are good—very good—and it is time to acknowledge and appreciate these solid relationships. As in any intimate relationship, stepdaughters and stepmothers face many challenges together, but they also share many precious experiences. In this book, I hope to show that there is much to cherish and celebrate in stepmother-stepdaughter relationships, though sometimes—as with many things in life—we see that only in retrospect.

In talking with stepmothers and stepdaughters about their experiences, it became clear that coming to each other from a place of love and respect is our greatest challenge—and the greatest gift we can offer each other. And, as I learned from these wise women, it is never too late to change and grow in our own perceptions of ourselves and of each other. It's never too late to give love or to let love into our hearts and lives.

My conversations with these women have given me a new perspective on and greater appreciation of my own experiences and relationships. I hope that reading their stories will do the same for you. I hope, too, that you will see what a gift your relationship with your stepmother or stepdaughter is. My wish for you is that this relationship, which began by chance, may become a friendship that lasts a lifetime.

Introduction

Stepmothers and stepdaughters are part of a growing familial reality. In the 1960s and 1970s, the rate of divorce began to increase substantially, to the point where today it is estimated that "approximately 60 percent of all first marriages will end in divorce."[1] Growing numbers of parents and children are therefore living in combined families. In fact, nuclear families are now the minority in today's ever-increasing diverse society.[2]

Although experts vary in their estimates of the number of children growing up in stepfamilies, everyone agrees that the number is significant. In their book *Stepmothers: Keeping It Together with Your Husband and His Kids,* Mary Bloch Jones and Jo Ann Schiller say that today "one out of four children in this country . . . lives with a stepparent by the age of sixteen...."[3] Others estimate that in the year 2000 "40 percent of all children will live with a stepparent,"[4] and "because children often travel back and forth between separated parents, many of these children will be part of more than one stepfamily."[5]

Whatever the actual numbers are, Jones and Schiller assert that "for better or worse, the traditional concept of the 'typical family,' with its clear-cut boundaries and mother, father, son. and daughter roles, no longer applies."[6] Those of us who live or have lived in combined situations know how true this statement is. Yet old ideas, understandings, and realities die slowly, even in the face of major demographical and sociological changes.

We are in the midst of a major evolution in the makeup and understanding of family life. In concrete, everyday terms, this means that stepfamilies are creating new ways of being family. Much of this creation has been experimental because, until relatively recently, few positive models of stepfamilies existed. Therefore, those of us in stepfamilies have been very literally finding our own way as we go.

The challenge of finding this way is complicated by the history of and stereotypes about stepparents, stepchildren, and stepfamilies. As Jane Nelson, Cheryl Erwin, and H. Stephen Glenn put it in their book *Positive Discipline for Blended Families*, "As recently as fifty years ago, stepfamilies formed primarily because an adult lost a spouse to death and eventually remarried. In fact, the 'step' in stepfamily and stepparent is commonly believed to come from an Old English term meaning 'bereaved.' Today, even though second and third marriages most commonly follow divorce, blended families are still families born out of pain and loss."[7] Harold H.

Bloomfield, M.D., comments on this further when he writes, "The word 'stepfamily' is associated with broken homes and deprivation. In fact, *stepchild* is defined by the *Random House Dictionary* not only as 'a child of a husband or wife by previous marriage,' but also as 'any person, organization, affiliate, or project that is not properly treated, supported, or appreciated.'"[8]

Given this cultural understanding of "stepness," it is not surprising that being a stepmother, a stepdaughter, or a stepfamily is such a difficult undertaking. Family life is a challenge in the very best of circumstances; the combining of families—with the extra emotional, logistical, and practical considerations that come along with it—makes it doubly so. But what is often ignored or unappreciated is that these families, which can be seen as a variation on the traditional extended family, can be healthy and good. Combining with its special challenges, also offers corresponding opportunities for growth and creativity as we learn about ourselves, others, and our relationships. In spite of these opportunities for growth and creativity, the step experience is at best a demanding one; at worst, it can be a very difficult and disappointing one.

The irony is that this whole experience begins with love. Because of the love she shares with a man, the stepmother opens her heart and her life to his children as well. By extension, her life is also tied to the mother of his children and more indirectly to the ex-wife's new family, if she has one. Given the circumstances, it is not surprising that new stepmothers often wonder just who and what they are; they find it difficult to adequately define themselves and their relationship with their stepchildren. They also often find themselves struggling to come to terms with themselves as "parents" who did not give birth to these children.

If defining one's identity is challenging, knowing how to act as a stepmother can be even more difficult. Many stepmothers declare that the keys to successful stepparenting are learning to let go, learning not to mother, and learning not to complain. The stepmother must somehow maintain a neutral position in relation to the raising of her stepchildren, yet still be loving and supportive of them, while also establishing appropriate behavioral boundaries. To say that stepmothers have a fine line to walk is an understatement. They must know when and when not to say things; they must know when and when not to act; they must know how and how not to blend in. Stepmothers know that they will never fully understand the step relationship, and yet they strive to do the best they can in a very challenging situation.

As they face the difficulties of stepmothering, many women seek to better understand themselves and those with whom they share their lives. Before self-help resources existed to assist them, stepmothers not only turned inward, but also sought guidance from friends who were stepmothers. In addition, some chose therapy to help sort out the myriad threads of stepmothering. With perseverance and a strong desire for a healthy, loving family life, stepmothers have found and created ways to thrive. These women are proud to be stepmothers—proud to have been there for their stepchildren and proud to have helped define "stepmother" in a new and positive way.

Unfortunately for others, the stepmothering experience is not only demanding, but also disappointing. According to Jones and Schiller, "Those who are disappointed universally say their presence in the family is resented and resisted by their stepchildren and that their husbands for a variety of reasons, lack the inclination or the power to improve the situation. Overall, the specific nature of the disappointment stepmothers experience falls into four main, sometimes overlapping, areas. First, . . . there are those that are surprised at how little appreciation or satisfaction they receive from their stepchildren for their efforts. Next, . . . some complain that they feel 'used' or 'invaded' by stepchildren who are basically 'lazy,' 'self-centered,' and 'greedy.' Third, stepmothers . . . are disappointed in their husband's inability or unwillingness to work with them to be supportive of them. Finally, . . . some women are 'ignored' or 'not recognized as individuals' to the point they feel resentful and 'invisible.'"[9]

There is no way of knowing how many stepmothers feel resentful, invisible, and deeply disappointed, but the emotional toll they pay is a heavy one. Support is crucial as they seek to cope with difficult family dynamics and struggle to maintain a healthy sense of self.

As with stepmothers, stepdaughters describe the step experience as either challenging yet fulfilling, or difficult and disappointing. The daily concerns of stepdaughters, however, not surprisingly are somewhat different than those of stepmothers.

Stepdaughters usually have two sets of parents and therefore must travel between two homes. As a result, many stepdaughters have to juggle two sets of "at home" rules. As children, they may have trouble adjusting to a new stepfamily dynamic, for example, where the rules are different and seem to restrict their independence. If they were latchkey children prior to their father's remarriage, and if their father's new wife does not work outside the home, suddenly having her there when they get home from school can feel like a major invasion. Stepchildren's response is often to resist that invasion. But for others, the presence of a stepmother provides a new kind of stability in their lives, one that they had been seeking.

Another challenging aspect of home life for step-daughters is making arrangements for holidays. Simply put, holidays can be extremely difficult for all family members. This is particularly true for children whose time must be split between the two homes of their parents. At a time of year when family togetherness, and most often *nuclear family* togetherness, is emphasized in the surrounding culture (TV, movies, commercials, and so on), holidays become a concrete reminder of the brokenness of their own family lives.

In addition to juggling their two-home situation, oftentimes stepdaughters also must face their parents' emotions and feelings toward each other, each other's new spouse, each other's stepchildren, and, of course, toward the daughters/stepdaughters themselves.

On top of their parents' emotional struggles, step-daughters face their own inner turmoil. A stepdaughter may feel threatened by this new "mother figure" and guilty about having a woman other than her mother in her life. She may wonder, now that her father has someone new to love, if he will continue to love her, especially if she has been "Daddy's girl." These emotions are joined, among others, by fears of abandonment as well as needs to be independent, loved, appreciated, and simply a child growing up.

Because stepdaughters can't please, love, or even like everyone in their new family configurations equally, they often feel deep guilt, which is compounded by the confusion they feel about their dad and mom not being together. Sadness, power struggles, and confrontations often grow out of these feelings of guilt and confusion.

Fortunately, though, stepdaughters often come to terms—sometimes earlier, sometimes later—with having a stepmother in their lives. When a stepdaughter sees that this woman is not just another one of Dad's dates, but rather that she is a permanent and stable part of her father's life, she is often able to give the stepmom a chance.

Whatever their own step experiences may be, few stepmothers or stepdaughters would claim that the stepfamily road is an easy one. Yet the women who participated in the interviews for this book talked honestly and courageously—of their blessings as well as their battle scars, their experiences of fulfillment as well as their disappointments, their joys as well as their sorrows. They have walked through the challenging circumstances of their lives with grace, confidence, and style, and they continue their efforts to show their stepmothers and stepdaughters how much they mean to them each day. This is a testimony to their openness of heart and their willingness to live lives of discovery, deepening, daring, and delight. These wonderful qualities are what I seek to affirm, appreciate, and celebrate in the pages that follow.

Discovery

Learning as We Go

Love starts it all. A woman and a man meet, fall in love, and choose to spend their lives together. Sounds simple, doesn't it? We know, of course, that love relationships are rarely that simple, and relationships where one or both partners have been married before, and have children, are not simple at all. But love is at the heart of it, and love can provide the hope, energy, and transformative power to meet the day-to-day challenges that lie ahead. That love will also, as all love does, have a lot of learning to do.

For future stepmothers, learning most likely begins when you find out that the man you are dating has children. He may find out that you have children too. Then what? You'll meet the children—and probably your special man's parents, other family members, and perhaps even his ex-wife. You'll learn to be yourself in situations in which you never expected to find yourself. You'll learn new ways of relating to children you did not give birth to. You will begin a new life together, a life for which there are few models and, unfortunately, often little support. You may, for the first time in your life, be labeled a "wicked stepmother" and wonder how that transformation occurred, when you're still the same old person you always were.

13

For future stepdaughters, you will discover that your father is serious about the woman he is dating. You will meet her and wonder, at worst, how you could ever live together, or, at best, how you ever could have lived without each other. Chances are that reality will fall somewhere in between. You'll learn how to live in a new family—with a new stepmother and perhaps new stepsiblings—and discover that stereotypes of the "wicked stepmother" and "evil stepdaughter" are not at all what they seem.

In this section, stepmothers and stepdaughters share stories about the early days of their relationships—getting to know each other, beginning their lives together, and wrestling with the always-present stereotypes. These are days of discovery and learning—about oneself, about others, and about loving and living in new ways.

Getting to Know You . . .
and You . . . and You

"Did you happen to mention that the dinner is your fiftieth birthday party and your entire family is going to be there?"

— STACEY, STEPDAUGHTER, AGE 32

In that delightful scene from Rodgers and Hammerstein's *The King and I,* Anna, the English schoolteacher, meets the children of the king of Siam—row after row of them—and sings breezily, "Getting to know you . . ." If only all initial encounters could go so easily! Perhaps your first encounter with that special man in your life did go easily, which is why you continued to see each other. But then there was that not-so-small detail of meeting his children.

Most of us can recall meeting the parents of a special man in our lives and how nerve-racking it was. Meeting children, especially potential stepchildren, can make us even more nervous. The same is true for children meeting a potential stepparent. It can be a delight, an ordeal, or something in between. Depending on a number of factors—individual personalities, the ages of

15

the children, their relationship with their parents, the amount of time that has passed since the divorce or death—there may be a great deal of tension or none at all. For potential stepmothers and stepchildren alike, nervousness or fear may mix with anticipation, curiosity with uncertainty, and confusion with hope as they prepare for their first meeting.

Clearly the first encounter with one's future stepchildren is a significant one. First impressions, for better or for worse, are often long lasting. They can, of course, be wonderful or terrible, valid or erroneous—or a mixture of these and any number of other responses. Bonding may take place immediately, or a foundation may be laid upon which the relationship will be built more slowly. For the woman and children entering into a new relationship, this initial meeting usually sets the tone for what is to come.

It's hard not to be nervous at a first meeting, and the desire to be liked and accepted is strong, both for children and adults. For stepmothers, trying too hard or acting unnaturally, however, will quickly be picked up by perceptive children. There are no guarantees that his children will like you, and to change who you are will only complicate matters—now and later. Though it is easier said than done (and easier for some women than others), it is best simply to be yourself, as Mary was in her first encounter with her soon-to-be stepfamily.

Mary, a fifty-five-year-old stepmother, recalled, "I met Jim in an airport in Puerto Vallarta. He asked me if he could call me the next time he traveled through Los Angeles, where I lived. To my surprise, he called the following Saturday, said he was coming to town, and asked if I would like to go to dinner with him."

For Mary, it was a lovely invitation—except that Jim had left out one very important detail. As Jim's daughter Stacey recalls, "When Dad told me he had scheduled a date with 'the most amazing woman' the following week, I asked him, 'Did you happen to mention that the dinner is your fiftieth birthday party and your entire family is going to be there?'"

Mary's first date with Jim thus became an extended family affair. Some less confident women might have folded when finding themselves in a situation like this, but Mary took it in stride.

"It was really something," Mary chuckled. "Jim had arranged for a limo to pick me up. When Jim and I got into the car, his two eldest daughters—Amy, who was twenty, and Stacey, who was twenty-two—were waiting inside. I liked them right away."

Future stepdaughters Amy and Stacey responded to Mary in a similar way. Amy remembers, "She just jumped right in and said, 'Hi, everybody!' Her comfort level was so amazing. She was totally herself. I loved her right from the get-go." Stacey agreed, "I loved Mary right from the beginning too. She was so comfortable with herself. Later, when she met the rest of the family, my dad's mother, his sister, and brother-in-law, I knew she would be one of the family."

Although Mary and Jim had an unusual first date, being with the entire family right off the bat was a great way for Mary to capture a real sense of the person she was getting involved with. "What I loved was the inter-action," Mary remembers. "I saw Jim as a father, a brother, and a son all in the same night. The first impression all the way around was so positive."

Like Mary's first impression of Jim and her future stepfamily, my first impression of my own future step-mother, Linda, was also positive. Fortunately, so was her impression of me! Here's what she remembers about meeting my father, John, and, a bit later, me: "I met John at a Fourth of July party and immediately knew we had something in common. That summer I was spend-ing most weekends at the pool of some good friends, so I invited John to meet my friends and bring his daugh-ter for a swim. Before they got there, I found myself worrying that she might be the evil child from hell who would get even with me for trying to come between her and her devoted daddy. In fact, it was an enjoyable, easy, instant bonding of two females who had this incredibly interesting male figure in common.

"Late in the day when I was standing at the car saying good-bye, Karen stuck her head out of the window and said, 'I just met you and don't really know you, but I wish you could come home with us.' I was hooked— you know, as in hook, line, and sinker."

Linda and I were fortunate in that we formed a mutual bond very quickly. That day was the first in the beginning of a twenty-five-year relationship, one that continued to grow from weekend mom and daughter to lifelong friends.

These early encounters, both first and subsequent ones, are often shaped in part by certain family dynamics. Every family, whether two people or ten, establishes its own set of habits, patterns, traditions, and schedules. The more limited the time together—as with noncustodial parents and children—the more deeply etched in stone those patterns are likely to become. A woman dating a divorced man who is actively involved with his children learns very quickly that some things will never interfere with his time with them. Because disruption of these routines can cause hostility and resentment, women wisely learn to handle these situations with care and compromise.

After a few midweek dates, Lou, a fifty-five-year-old

stepmother, discovered just how serious the weekly dad-and-daughter ritual was. She remembers, "Don would pick Eleanor up at her mother's house every Saturday morning and return her Sunday night. Very early on I discovered that his time with Eleanor was sacred. It became a part of my weekly ritual too. Don and I made dates during the week, but if I wanted to join in on a weekend outing with him and Eleanor, I always knew I was welcome."

Not all beginnings start off as smoothly as those of stepmothers Mary, Linda, and Lou. Often a woman encounters stepchildren whose experience with a previous stepmother was less than positive. An earlier negative relationship with the children can get things off to a rocky start, though that isn't always the case, as Susan learned.

Susan, a fifty-year-old stepmother, met Kelly, the daughter of the man she was dating, when Kelly was nineteen years old. She was an extremely troubled young girl with a history of drug abuse and a volatile relationship with her father's second wife. Susan remembered, "My first impression was that this girl was a piece of work. I knew she had a history of behavioral and emotional troubles, so I approached Kelly in a warm, friendly way. I think she loved me right off the bat."

Just as Lou recognized the importance of the father-daughter connection in Eleanor's relationship with her dad, Gloria, forty-four, also recognized early on how important that connection was for her future step-daughter, Stephanie. Like Susan's stepdaughter, Kelly, Stephanie had some significant problems. While dating Stephanie's dad, Richard, Gloria encouraged him to bring Stephanie back into his life. Gloria saw the writing on the wall. As she put it, "What I saw was a young girl desperate for a family unit because she had never recovered from the loss of her family. She was living in her car, selling and using drugs. When I met my future husband, he was looking to buy a place and I said, 'You have to buy something that will allow you to live with your daughter.' I readily accepted her. I knew that if I cared about this man, and I did, that I would have to clear the waters with Stephanie."

Early in her relationship with her future husband, Gloria strongly advocated for Stephanie's needs. When meeting their future husband's child for the first time, other women may feel themselves entering a kind of limbo—unable to really get involved in decisions concerning the child and yet seeing things they would like to change. Forever aware of the mother's presence, they realize they need to tread lightly.

Lynda, age fifty-three, remembers meeting her future stepdaughter, Beth, for the first time: "Before I was

21

married to my husband, we flew to New York where his children, a boy and a girl, were living with their mother. We picked up the kids and took them to Rockefeller Center. When I first laid eyes on Beth, I thought she was the most adorable thing I had ever seen. She was so cute, even though her hair was in her face, her hat was crooked, and her coat was buttoned wrong. I thought, 'Who would let their child leave the house that way?'— especially if they knew they were going out with family. I took one look at her and wanted to clean her up."

Despite her initial inclination, Lynda knew it wasn't appropriate at that time for her to get involved. Eventually she would play a very significant, though challenging, role in Beth's life, but at that early stage, it was just time for them to get to know each other.

Beth also remembers the day when she and Lynda met. "When Dad and Lynda came to pick up my brother and me, I just looked at them and smiled. Even though I was very young, I'd learned to act very adult-like—and lovable."

Though their initial meeting was positive, Beth and Lynda would have some very difficult times in later years, when Beth's long-repressed anger would flare up. That day in New York, when Lynda and Beth met for the first time, neither one of them could have imagined the challenges—and the joys—that lay ahead.

Like Lynda and Beth, Suzanne and her stepmother, Liz, could not have imagined what the future held for them. In Suzanne and Liz's case, however, their relationship was hard from the start.

Suzanne was just six years old when she met Liz. Suzanne remembers, "I was so young when my stepmother came into my life. I didn't know what to make of it. My parents were bitter with each other, and my sister and I got caught in the middle. I would see Liz on the weekends when I would visit my father. She wanted me to like her and I tried, but the truth is, I just didn't like her. To me, she was the woman who had divided my family." It would be many years before Suzanne would experience a reconciliation with Liz.

Like Liz, Karla, thirty-nine, would eventually come to play a significant role in her stepdaughter's life after some difficult times. But unlike Liz and Suzanne's early relationship, Karla and Melanie's was light, carefree, and playful.

Karla, a thirty-nine-year-old stepmother, met her stepdaughter, Melanie, when she was five or six. Karla recalls, "Before I started dating her dad, I would see her occasionally at church. She was cute and fun and I would play games with her. Her dad didn't have her very often, but after we started dating, I would see her whenever he did."

23

Some women like Diane, who is now a fifty, feel unprepared going into the step relationship. When Diane met Lisa, a sweet little four-year-old, she recalls that her first impression was very positive: "I met her when I was twenty-four years old. I had never been married. I thought Lisa was very cute, sweet, and a nice little girl, but I was not at all prepared for doing much. Going into this relationship, I thought, 'Well, I like kids and this will be fun.' I had been dating Lisa's father for a couple of years. He was doing his parenting long distance. When I came on the scene, I changed the dynamic. I soon became a stepmom and had absolutely no idea what I was doing."

Some women don't even think about being prepared or unprepared to be a stepmother, and they jump right into their new role with the innocence of a child. Twenty-nine-year-old Caroline, a stepmother of two and a mother of two, couldn't be more positive about her unique beginning with her stepchildren. "I've been a stepparent for five and half years, and have been with my husband for nine, total. We didn't live together before we got married, but we did everything together with his kids."

According to Caroline, hanging out with her boyfriend's kids, Ashley and Austin, was like hanging out with younger brothers and sisters. "When I first met

Mark," she said, "I was twenty. When he told me he was divorced and he had two small children, I was very excited. I said, 'Oh, let's take them to Disneyland!' That was our first meeting. We got along great because I was probably just as silly as they were. They were really warm and receptive to me. I had a wonderful day with them and I really looked forward to our next adventure."

Caroline's first encounter with the children was not as a mother figure. She explains, "I walked in as somebody fun. I didn't walk in and start telling them what to do. Maybe I was kind of naive—I didn't look at the big picture of what I was getting myself into. I just thought, 'This guy is great. He has these great kids and I'm having fun.'"

New relationships bring happiness with them and the happiness that stepdaughters often notice is that of their fathers. Amy, who met her future stepmother in a limo on her father's fiftieth birthday, remembers warmly, "When I saw Mary squeezing my dad's hand, I could just tell this was it." Zanetha, a thirty-one-year-old stepdaughter, also has warm memories of her first meeting with her future stepmother, Joi. Zanetha says, "When my sister and I first met Joi, we saw our dad smile more than he ever had. It was obvious that he was so in love with her."

First encounters and the initial stages of getting to

know each other can be fun, challenging, heart-warming, and sometimes uncertain. The process of discovering and learning continues long after those early days, when stepmothers, stepdaughters, and their whole families eventually begin their daily lives together.

Beginning Our Lives Together

*"When we did our ring ceremony, we had
gold rings for Ashley and Austin. . . .
Mark and I were not just marrying each
other; we were* all *marrying each other."*

—CAROLINE, STEPMOTHER, AGE 29

For most soon-to-be stepdaughters and stepmothers, there is a certain amount of transition time that passes prior to the event that marks a singular change in both their lives. In some cases, the transition will occur relatively quietly. In other cases, a big wedding marks the official beginning of life together.

Those women who have wedding celebrations agree that including the children in their special day makes all the difference in kicking off a healthy, harmonious beginning. With the stepchildren present, it not only brings the whole family together, but it also reassures stepchildren that they will not be excluded from this new family. At the time the wedding vows are exchanged, the children literally see a new family emerge. A celebration of the joining of lives is a positive beginning, and hopefully a harbinger of happy days ahead.

In my own case, when the big day came around for Linda and my father, John, I felt included and loved. They asked me to be the flower girl, which seemed so grown up. I felt important and special.

The wedding preparations were exciting. As a girl of ten, wearing a pretty dress and getting my hair done with all the other women was my first real taste of what being a woman was about. My mother helped me pick out my dress and shoes, and she took me to the house way up in the hills of Los Angeles for the beautiful garden wedding. As soon as it was over, I threw petals everywhere and hugged everyone.

As wonderful as the day was, there were also a couple of sad moments—when Mom didn't stay with me for the wedding and when Dad and Linda prepared to leave on their honeymoon. I didn't understand why Mom couldn't be with me, and then why Dad and Linda were leaving me behind. In the midst of chaos, with friends and family buzzing around, Linda took me in her arms and comforted me. She assured me that I was a part of this very special celebration and that, even though I couldn't go with them, I was loved and wanted.

I knew this was the beginning of a new family, which was in addition to the one I had with my mother and stepfather. I wasn't aware, however, of the ramifications of this—two homes, two holiday dinners, two birthday parties, and so on—but I was certain that I was loved, not only by my father and mother but also by my stepmother and stepfather.

Many women consciously strive to include children in their weddings as a way of beginning their life together in a positive way. Caroline was exuberant when I asked about this pivotal time in her life.

"When Mark and I got married," Caroline shared, "we had a big wedding in a big church with a big reception. I wore the full white traditional wedding gown. Austin was Mark's junior groomsman and Ashley was my junior bridesmaid. When we did our ring ceremony, we had gold rings for Ashley and Austin as well. We exchanged rings and talked about these rings as symbolic of the bonding of our family. The officiant explained that Mark and I were not just marrying each other, we were *all* marrying each other. That was the only way we wanted to do it."

Caroline paused, then added, "We had so many people say that the exchanging of the rings was the most beautiful thing they had ever witnessed. It was never just our wedding day. It was a celebration of our new family together."

When Kathy married David, Rhonda, his mature fourteen-year-old daughter, added to the joy of their wedding day when she put this message for her father and new stepmother on tape: "Hi, Kathy. Hi, Dad. I just want to tell you, I'm happy you guys are married. Kathy, I'm so happy you're my mom. You make a great couple, and I know you're meant to be together. I love you both so much. This is the happiest day of my life."

Kathy commented, "Rhonda had said to me that she was so sad when her mom and dad had divorced, but she knew that if they hadn't, I would never have become her stepmother." That hard loss made it possible for this special new relationship to come into existence. Shaking her head, Kathy added, "It all was just amazing."

For others, the beginning of life together can be much more quick and subtle. We met Diane in the last chapter as she met her first stepdaughter, Lisa. Diane eventually divorced Lisa's father. When she remarried, she gained a second stepdaughter, Ariel. "Our first meeting took place at my house," Diane remembered. "Ariel came over with Mike, her father, on the spur of the moment. Ariel is one of the world's nicest people. She's very sociable. I had heard so much about her and after she came to visit, she decided she wanted to stay at my house. That day we emptied out my study and moved her things in.

"From that point on," Diane continued, "when she was visiting her father, she would stay at my place in

Wisconsin. She and her mom are so close. I know the strength of character it took for such a young girl to not only initiate the first meeting with me, but then to make the difficult choice to move away from her mother who lived in California. And she did this for the sake of her own well-being, to be near her friends, who meant a great deal to her. She moved in full time after she left California. A few months later Mike and I bought a new house together and we were married. So my son, Jamie, Ariel, Mike, and myself all lived together."

Many stepmothers soon become mentors to their new stepdaughters. Instead of "mothering," stepmothers may act as a "neutral" figure, one who is not as quick to judge or react. A stepdaughter may let the stepmother into her life in a way that she doesn't even extend to her mother. Such was the case with Susan and her stepdaughter, Kelly.

When Susan and Kelly's father moved into their own home together, Kelly moved in too, along with Susan's children. Susan recalls, "Then I had to deal with this new crisis that was growing out of Kelly's emotional problems. What made the difference was that I was able to talk to her. My husband says I am one of the few people who can talk to Kelly, so when I sat down with my guidelines, it went well. I don't sweat the small stuff, but if she did something big, I called her on it.

31

"Step by step, I encouraged Kelly to reach another level. I encouraged her to stick with something. With a lot of love from her father and from me, she slowly but surely started pulling herself out of her depression."

Sue, fifty years old, also remembers a kind of freedom that came with being a stepmother to Cathleen, rather than a mother. "I think Cathleen really appreciated having someone who was in her corner, who didn't have to be the primary disciplinarian," explained Sue. "Because of that, we were able to talk. I took her to lunch one time when she was about twelve and asked her question after question. After about an hour and a half she said, 'Whew! I've never talked so much in my life!' That was the starting point of a relationship in which we could really share on a much deeper level than ever before. In those years I think I was a person with whom she could talk about what was going on in her life, but I also was a person who was a haven for her—she got an awful lot of attention from me."

New relationships between stepdaughters and stepmothers can deepen quickly, especially when a crisis arises. A stepdaughter, when hesitant about approaching her mother or father about a serious problem, may seek out the stepmother, as one who can listen and give advice. Early in her relationship with her stepdaughter, Stephanie, Gloria became such a sounding board.

"My approach," Gloria said about her early days with Stephanie, "was very nonthreatening. Because of that, when she became pregnant six months later, I was the first person she came to. She was terrified of her mother and father, so she came to me. I told her, 'I'll never be your mother, I'll never be anything other than a friend.' I helped her overcome her trepidation and encouraged her to tell her parents. She was so out of control that if I had come down too heavily on her, I would have lost her. I think she knew then that if I didn't judge her about this, I wouldn't judge her about anything. Her coming to me sealed our relationship."

Generosity of heart, as Gloria offered Stephanie, provides a strong foundation for new stepmother-step-daughter relationships. Monica, now thirty-one, recalls a particularly precious memory in her early relationship with her stepmother: "It was soon after my dad and my stepmother, Leah, were married. Leah, my twin sister, and I were out together shopping. I was randomly going through a department store and I saw this sewing machine. I said to Leah, 'Wouldn't it be great to learn how to sew?' A few days later, Leah surprised my sister and me with this sewing machine. I know she didn't have the money. She did it out of the goodness of her heart. She simply knew I would appreciate it. She gave my sister and me each our own patterns, she bought the scissors, needles, thread, everything I needed. I was so shocked! I couldn't believe how much she cared."

As families combine, they also extend. Not only do they bring together father, stepmother, children, and stepchildren, they also gather in grandparents, aunts, uncles, and others. This larger family can play an integral role in supporting and affirming new combinations of family relationships.

Susan explained how her own immediate family has been a positive influence on her new, combined family: "I have a very loving and very accepting small family. My mother took my stepdaughter, Kelly, in right away. My stepchildren were always included in everything."

This level of acceptance also extended to Susan's new husband. Susan recalls, "It wasn't 'your kids,' 'my kids.' When my kids started acting up—they were holy terrors—it was my husband's turn to support me. He has been wonderful. He's the rock. My husband and I both agree that the love within our family has kept us going through all of our hard times."

Women like Diane, Sue, Gloria, Susan, and Leah became stepmothers when they had a certain measure of maturity and experience in life. That maturity and experience enabled them to be present for their step-daughters in a way that might not have been possible if they had become stepmothers at a much younger age. The demands on very young women who become step-mothers are daunting.

Renée remembers, "I was fifteen and pregnant with her dad's baby, but it didn't occur to me that Louise would really have anything to do with our lives. I knew this was his daughter, but all I could think about was having my own family. I didn't think once about what it would be like to have to deal with another child, some-one else's child. It was a rude awakening."

Regardless of whether their personal experience was smooth and easy or rocky and difficult, all the women I interviewed believe that a beautiful and long-lasting relationship is possible if the stepmother and step-daughter put aside their personal fears and agendas. Coming together with as few presumptions as possible allows the relationship to grow naturally and opens up possibilities for a rich and rewarding life together. Often one of the first expectations to be put aside is that the new stepmom will turn out to be the stereotypical "wicked stepmother."

Ditching the Wicked Stepmother

"If I could change the term 'wicked stepmother' to anything, I would choose 'fairy godmother.'"

—JENNIFER, STEPDAUGHTER, AGE 27

I remember when my mom and my stepmother, Linda, took me to the mall to buy my prom dress. I introduced them to my friends as "my mom" and, in a teasing tone, "my wicked stepmom." My friends were dumbfounded. How could I actually be shopping with them both—*together!* At that time, stepfamilies were not as prevalent as they are today, and it was very unusual to see a mom and stepmom getting along, much less shopping together.

My mom, Linda, and I—as part of my healthy, functioning, combined family—got a kick out of seeing people's reactions of amazement, confusion, and disbelief. Though these responses were funny on the one hand, on the other hand, they were most definitely were not funny because we encountered them so frequently. People's responses were, and still remain, a testimony to the power of the "wicked stepmother" myth.

As is often the case in situations of high stress, humor becomes a way of coping. Though Mom, Linda, and I didn't feel the stress in our own relationship, we did feel the stress *on* it—in the form of the negative expectations and disbelief of others. Humor was not only a way to fend off those negative responses and disbelief, but also our way of unconsciously saying, "Hey, lighten up, would you? Look what's right in front of you—a healthy, combined family. We exist—and we get along very well, thanks!"

That kind of analysis only comes in retrospect. At the time, I never felt uncomfortable. We had a good time with people's responses, and we never took it personally. Our relationship was positive, so it wasn't an issue for us. We definitely were a rare breed of family. I know that in growing up with love and understanding from both of these women (not to mention the fact that they enjoyed each other's company), I was not living in the average "step" scenario. And although I felt a degree of separation because of this, I was proud of our family and felt very loved.

For most of the women I interviewed, however, the stereotypes do create problems. Over 80 percent disapproved of the term "wicked stepmother" and confirmed that it has had a negative effect on them. For those striving to be good stepmothers, the "wicked stepmother" myth is disheartening at best and outright destructive at worst. For those learning to be good stepdaughters, the myth supports the idea that there is something shameful and dysfunctional about combined families, and it blatantly demonizes stepmothers—those women who love and care for their nonbiological children.

Caroline reflected, "I told my kids a long time ago that I didn't like the word 'stepmom'—as associated with the term 'the wicked stepmother.' I hated that. It makes me feel like I am this horrible, awful person. What I have tried to explain to them is that I'm not just here because I married their dad. 'I tell them, I'm here because I want to be. I'm here because I love you like my own. We are a family and I want to be with you.'"

Cherie, a fifty-two-year-old stepdaughter, thinks many women have had to fight the negative stereotype: "Look how many people resent the 'wicked stepmother' label. Just the word 'stepmother' has such a negative connotation. You hardly ever hear anybody speak glowingly in terms of their step-anything."

Not only stepmothers are affected by this damaging myth. It reaches down through the generations—even to stepgrandchildren. Sherry, also fifty-two years old and a stepdaughter, stepmother, and stepgrandmother, said, "Jennifer, my stepdaughter, was talking about me being the 'wicked stepmom' with her children. The youngest child had a fit and the daughter screamed, 'She is not, she is not! I love Sherry.'"

Given the negative connotations of the pervasive "wicked stepmother" myth, it's not surprising that stepmothers themselves are sometimes a little uncertain how to refer to themselves. For many, the word "step" is vague and confers a certain coldness to a relationship that is much more personal and refined. Because of this impersonality and its frequent misinterpretation, women like Patti resent it and avoid the term all together.

"Stepmother is a scary word," Patti, a fifty-five-year-old stepmother, told me. Then with more vehemence she added, "I'm *not* a stepmother! I'm their father's wife. I'm not their mother. I am in no way their mother, and so what does stepmother really mean? Step means once removed, right? But I'm not removed from anything."

Karla, age thirty-nine, has created her own interpretation of stepmother, which communicates her sense of its meaning. It is her stepdaughter, Melanie, who has difficulty with the word, especially since Karla and Melanie's father divorced.

Karla explained, "To me stepmother means being a friend and a mother. That's really what I am to Melanie. Although we are friends, I am absolutely a motherly friend. After my divorce, Melanie didn't know how to introduce me. I told her it would be silly to say 'This is my friend,' because that is not our relationship. I am her stepmother, but I think Melanie did have some negative feelings about it."

Beyond the "wicked" connotations, there is the reality that many people think of the role of stepmother as inconsequential. Kathy, a twenty-nine-year-old stepmother, explained, "I feel that most people see being a stepmother as a somewhat insignificant role. If you're a stepmom, you have that role simply through marriage. There are times when you may look or feel like you don't matter. After all, do you really have any say on anything? You're just the stepparent, the stepmother, right? You don't have any rights to this family and its growth."

For Kathy, and for many others such as Caroline, that understanding of stepmother is dead wrong. "When I said my vows, 'till death do us part,' that's what I meant," Caroline asserted. "Just because I'm a stepmom doesn't mean that I'm not here for the long haul. I'm here in the same way I would be had I given birth to these children. I accepted them as a part of my life. I look at them the same way I look at my own kids."

In most cases, stepmothers are not trying to replace the mother. As Frances put it, "The mother is first and foremost their mother. I will never try to take her place. She has created a sacred role with them. I have said to the kids from day one, 'I never want to take your mother's place. She is your mother and you love her, and I will always support that.' I wouldn't have a problem if they said, 'This is my second mom' or something of that nature to describe my place because I have a great relationship with them, but I can see where some people might still be apprehensive about that: 'Oh, does that mean you're saying I'm second in line?'"

As we try to ditch the "wicked stepmother" myth, perhaps those who speak most eloquently against it and for the new reality of stepmothers are the stepdaughters who have been raised and nurtured by stepmothers.

As Becky, a stepdaughter in her twenties, put it, "I have two mothers, I don't have one. I don't call my stepmother 'Mom,' I call her 'Teresa,' but I feel like she's extra. Teresa's daughter only has one mom. I have two."

"It's a relationship that's based on fun, but with guidelines," Jennifer, a twenty-seven-year-old stepdaughter, said. "That's what Sherry did with us—fun mixed with balance. She never said, 'I'm going to run and tell your dad.' She never felt so frustrated that she had to do that. I think she had great patience with us, because we really gave it to her. There were four of us children against her alone. If I could change the term 'wicked stepmother' to anything, I would choose 'fairy godmother.' That's what Sherry was for us."

Zanetha first heard of the wicked "step-thing" when she discovered she would be a stepdaughter. Falling into that role at seventeen, Zanetha was amazed that the relationship was nothing like she had envisioned it. She said, "My stepmother has always been Mama Joi—since day one. I introduce her as 'my mama, Joi' when I meet people. They see she is joyous and exudes this energy, and then it makes all the sense in the world. Since I became a stepdaughter, I've only heard negative things about the stepmother-stepdaughter relationship. However, since my father and Joi have been married, those issues have never surfaced for me."

Like Zanetha's experience, my own relationship with Linda provides inspiration and an energy that has only been positive. Our relationship has only gotten better with time—as has Deena's relationship with her step-mother, Patti. "I've respected her from the first day," thirty-two-year-old Deena said. "Every year I get to know a deeper layer of my stepmother. She's an amazing woman. 'Step' doesn't mean a step up or a step down. It means another mother figure, another addition to the family."

And finally, as twenty-three-year-old Ariel so eloquently explained, "Like an extra parent, a stepmother is another person in my life to learn and grow from; another person whom I can love and who will always love me; another person who is there for me through thick and thin. A stepmother is another person with whom I can share my love."

As these stepdaughters so clearly attest, it is loving, caring stepmothers themselves who, consciously or unconsciously, destroy the old stereotype. Through them, the old adage "actions speak louder than words" is proven true. Their actions and their lives prove that the "wicked stepmother" is dead.

Deepening

Facing the
Challenges of
Life Together

After those initial encounters and early days, stepmothers and stepdaughters move more deeply into the daily intricacies of life together. If there was a "honeymoon" period in the new relationship, that is now over. Change becomes reality as lives, homes, and children blend into a new way of being.

Change, of course, is not necessarily bad, but it is, well, change, and it affects everything. The love that brings a man and a woman together now must be balanced with the ordinariness of life. Perhaps a new home must be purchased, bedrooms allotted, house rules established, parental visits scheduled, and so on. All of this comes on top of the normal activities of life—work, school, meals, housework, and extracurricular pursuits.

Change comes, too, in how family members relate to one another—father to daughter, stepmother/stepfather to stepchildren. Tensions and difficulties may arise that lower expectations of what this new life together will be, but hope remains that such challenges can be worked through. At the same time, connections may solidify as once wide gaps begin to be bridged in surprising ways.

In this section, stepmothers and stepdaughters share stories of coping with changes. Some tell of lowering their initial expectations for their new families while still holding on to hope that true family closeness may eventually emerge. They also describe the unexpected yet gracious ways that stepmothers bridge the gaps in family relationships, especially between old families and new. These are days of deepening commitment, as stepmothers, stepdaughters, and their families learn to live together.

Changing, Changing,
Everything's Changing

*"She's getting rid of everything . . .
the artwork, the dog, everything!"*

—DEENA, STEPDAUGHTER, AGE 32
(QUOTING HER FATHER)

Change can be exhilarating, but it can also be confusing. Change opens us up to new possibilities, but it also makes us vulnerable. Whenever divorce or death is followed—either quickly or after a period of time—by a new relationship, marriage, and new family life, the emotional and practical repercussions are extensive. Practical considerations mingle with emotional issues, which frequently predominate, especially since anger and grief linger after divorce or death.

In new home configurations, stepmothers and stepdaughters, as well as other family members, must identify their roles and establish mutually acceptable boundaries. Differences in personalities, ages, expectations, hopes, and ways of doing things, can, at best, stimulate excitement about new possibilities and opportunities. At worst, they invoke hostility and resentment.

The addition of even one person in a relationship—for example, the birth of a child—can drastically change family dynamics. The addition of two or more affects the dynamics exponentially. The givens of family life are gone. What will take their place? Who will each person be and become? How will each person cope?

When Erika, now twenty-three, came to California with her brother to live with her father and stepmother, Joanna, she faced a challenging and confusing home situation. Not only did she have to live with her stepmother, whom she had only visited briefly, she also had to learn how to live with her stepsister, Tina. "We didn't know how to be sisters," Erika says now. "We were both jealous of what the other represented. Tina, who had all kinds of clothes and material possessions, reminded me of everything I didn't have as a child growing up at my mom's. And to Tina, my brother and I were exotic because we came from the East Coast. She resented that she wasn't part of that world." Erika and Tina, along with the rest of the family, experienced much pain and turmoil before they settled into a relatively peaceful coexistence as stepsisters.

Melanie, a stepdaughter in her thirties, admits that she was a spoiled only child, with her dad at her beck and call. Her father's remarriage was difficult for her, especially when Karla, her new and very young stepmother, quickly became pregnant. At eight years old, Melanie's whole world turned upside-down and she often threw tantrums to get attention.

"I was too young to fully comprehend the change, but I was very excited after Karla's first baby was born. I wanted to be a part of the family, and I still wanted to see my dad all the time. Now being a mother of three, I realize how difficult it must have been for Karla when I was there."

Melanie recalls that she would push and push until she got her way. She would find herself at her father's house with Karla and the new baby. For newlywed Karla, having an infant to care for as well as an insensitive, melodramatic child was too much to handle.

Karla, who is now thirty-nine years old and has five children (all born before she was twenty-five), admits having very mixed emotions about Melanie. Being young and immature, she had not anticipated the realities of having a stepchild. She did not look at Melanie as a family member nor did she want her to be one. She wanted a "perfect family," and that did not include a difficult, needy child from her husband's previous marriage.

The reality of Melanie's presence, however, forced Karla to keep pushing herself, though it wasn't easy. Not seeing Melanie as a part of her perfect-family picture, Karla resented having to invite her to birthday parties and other family events, but she always did because she couldn't bear to hurt Melanie's feelings. Despite the deep emotional strain it caused, Karla always tried to make choices that would include, rather than exclude, Melanie. She struggled to be a better, less jealous, more giving person, and made changes in her life accordingly.

Thirty-two-year-old Louise's situation was very similar to Melanie's. Her stepmother, Renée, soon grew tired of Louise's tireless tantrums and bouts for attention. Whenever Louise wasn't allowed to go to her dad's house, she would get her mom involved and start a conflict. This, as Louise told me, was a conscious way of getting what she wanted.

The change brought challenges that not only affected Louise's life and that of Renée and Louise's father, but they also affected her mother, with whom she lived part of the time. Louise would hear endless struggles pertaining to her visits. "I don't care what's going on with your new wife. I don't care about your new baby. You still have this daughter," her mother would yell. "Your relationship with her isn't going to change just because you decide to get married and have another baby."

In such times of great upheaval, it is important that parents and stepparents work diligently to maintain a regular, stable home life for the children. At all ages, the need for security and love is a priority. For a daughter who has been "Daddy's little girl" like Melanie or Louise were, a new woman can be threatening, especially if the daughter has been living with her father. The daughter can feel pushed out, desperate, and alone.

After speaking to several women who had found themselves in this type of situation, it became clear that the future of the relationship depends on how the stepmother treats the stepdaughter at this crucial time. If behavioral boundaries can be established and the lines of communication kept open, positive relationships can eventually grow. The challenge for the stepmother is to find a way to settle into the relationship without telling the daughter what to do and without trying to control her. Once the stepmother feels secure in her new role, she can make it clear that she's not there to break up or change the father-daughter relationship, but to love her husband without getting in the way of the daughter loving her father.

Deena, stepdaughter of Patti, recalled some early changes that made her fearful of losing her relationship with her father. After experiencing a very difficult time with her father's second wife several years before, Deena experienced trepidation when her father became engaged to Patti just months after he met her. Later, her father called her in a panic and her anxiety increased. 'She's getting rid of everything. All of it!' my dad said frantically. 'I came into the house and all the furniture was gone, including the artwork, the dog, everything!'

"I was fifteen years old when Dad went through a divorce from his second wife," Deena explained. "Those pieces of furniture and artwork had been what my dad and I had acquired during the years when the two of us had lived alone together. My concern wasn't really about the material stuff going out the door; I was more worried about my relationship with my father going out the door. That fear, however, was very short-lived because Patti made it known right away that she was not going to jeopardize my relationship with my father."

Deena continued, "I see now that getting rid of all that stuff was the right thing for Patti to do. It was hard initially, but it was part of this change process that I had to undergo. When I saw that my dad was happy for the first time in so long, it wasn't as difficult for me."

Changes in some families can become so disruptive that they may necessitate outside assistance. Like many women's experience as stepmothers, fifty-three-year-old Margaret's was hard work at first. Margaret shared, "My stepdaughter was torn between two families. When she came to visit us during the summers, she had a lot of animosity toward me. I think she thought I was going to take her dad away from her. It was at this time, I started going to therapy, and my therapist helped me tremendously in figuring out how to deal with Debbie."

No simple answers exist about how to effectively deal with the changes brought about when families merge together. Sometimes we stumble toward doing the right things, as Karla did by continuing to include Melanie in her family's life, even though she resented it at the time. Sometimes a seemingly hurtful action brings us to a surprising positive place, as Deena discovered after Patti did some unexpected spring cleaning. At other times, the best thing we can do, as Margaret did, is to seek help and advice from someone we trust.

As scary as changes are, and as much as the thought of being a stepmother or a stepdaughter may terrify us, communication breeds strong relationships. Doing what we know is best for the other person, even though it is difficult for us, and being willing to seek help, bring us closer together. Sometimes, though, when relationships are particularly difficult, we may find that it is simply necessary to lower our expectations, even while we hope for the best. The stories in the next chapter reflect this tension.

Lowering Expectations/
Holding on to Hope

*"Acceptance occurs when trust is built.
The stepmother-stepdaughter relationship
needs time to season."*

—ELEANOR, STEPDAUGHTER, AGE 32

One of the most difficult challenges of any relationship, is the balance between knowing when to push through difficulties and when to let go. We often enter our new relationships with high hopes and expectations. It's disheartening to let go of these, but sometimes that is the only viable response in a troubled stepmother-stepdaughter relationship. While lowering expectations and letting go may mean the end of some relationships, it may mark a new beginning for others. Throughout it all, as hard as it may be at times, we continue to hold on to our hope that someday we will come out on the other side with a deeper understanding and respect for each other as well as a renewed and loving relationship.

Some relationships force a lowering of expectations from the beginning. Sherry, a stepmother, who also has been a stepdaughter for over twenty-five years, faced such a situation when she became involved with the husband of a friend.

"Both of us were married when we met," Sherry said, "so it was very hard. There was a lot of anger and anxiety from all the spouses and all the kids. I knew his children—they went to the same school as my kids. I never had any idea that they were going to be my stepchildren.

"Early in our relationship, his kids—ages thirteen, eleven, and seven visited us every week because their mom was going through a difficult time. Because of the situation, they were very threatened by me," Sherry remembered.

In Sherry's case, her personality—ironically, her natural tendency to nurture—also played a part in the tensions between her and her husband's children. Sherry continued, "They definitely didn't look at me as another mother, although, when they were with me, I felt like I was their mother. When they thought I was trying to mother them, they would say, 'You're not my mom. Don't act like you are. Don't be nice to me.' It was hard for me. All I wanted to do was protect them. I am very nurturing, and taking care is what I love to do. It's a part of who I am as a person."

Eventually, Sherry faced that fact that her love and nurturing would not necessarily win all of the children over. "It got to the point that my husband's youngest daughter was very verbal about how much she disliked me," Sherry recalled. "When Sally saw me she would say, 'I hate it when you kiss me. Don't ever kiss me again. Don't hug me when I come over here.' I came to the realization we might never become close. Sadly, we finally stopped seeing her."

Children must struggle to realize that Dad—and Mom—are only human and have needs of their own. In many situations, as in Sherry's, the father must find a way to support both his children, who may be resisting his new relationship, and his wife, who must juggle dealing with his children as well as her own emotional needs. Yet, with time, mutual respect may develop. Stepchildren choose when they are ready to make the effort of building a new relationship. They cannot be pushed or pulled. They will forgive and accept when ready. Stepmothers told me that they saw the best results when they did not try to "mother" or "best-friend" the children into liking them. As Eleanor, a thirty-two-year-old stepdaughter, put it, "Acceptance occurs when trust is built. The stepmother-stepdaughter relationship needs time to season, as does the relationship with all stepchildren."

Many stepdaughters feel the need to flex their own muscles. Those stepdaughters I interviewed found that when a stepmother allowed her stepdaughter to find her way into the relationship at her own pace, the results were positive. This letting go reflects a mutual respect, which enables the stepmother-stepdaughter relationship to flourish and grow.

Becky, Teresa's twenty-seven-year-old stepdaughter, maintains that her stepmother's greatest strength has been her ability to not necessarily expect something in return for what she has given. Becky remembered, "She was giving to me, but she didn't push me to give her something back. There were times my siblings and I hurt her feelings, but she never chose to do that to us. I don't know how she did it. That's her incredible personality." In Teresa's case, her hopes for a better relationship were eventually realized, at least in part, by allowing things to take their own course. At times it may be a challenge to hold on to hope. Yet it is hope that sustains perseverance in difficult situations.

Lynda, age fifty-three, knows that her greatest strength in regard to her stepdaughter, Beth, has been that she has never abandoned all hope. "There were moments when I temporarily gave up," she said. "We have experienced the worst of times and the best of times. It was more than difficult. Our strength is that we have always kept going and tried to make it better through the good and the bad."

Some women such as Margaret take steps toward

more positive relationships by enlisting the help of a therapist. Therapy gave Margaret the skills to cope with the daily challenges and to maintain hope as well. "Without therapy, I do not know how I would have gotten through the whole twenty years. It steered me through all the ups and the downs. It changed my family's life."

The lowering of expectations also extends to stepmothers themselves. They must come to release their own expectations that they should be perfect mothers, should always know what's best, and should always be right. Sarah comments on this: "I was a new stepmother dealing with two emotionally disturbed children. My therapist helped me tremendously in figuring out how to cope with them. The kids and I had our share of yelling and screaming, but I took action and made it work. I think my stepdaughter, Brenda, knows that I have always been there for her and that we made it through, despite the fact that we all made mistakes. I make a point of acknowledging to her when I haven't been right—and I apologize."

Even after years of being in relationship with stepchildren, lowering expectations may still, unfortunately, be necessary. Sherry said, "My stepchildren are not really good about how they share their love, and I'm really quite sensitive. One stepdaughter said something like, 'Well, you're just Sherry.' She meant it in a loving way, as in I'm 'just Sherry' instead of her stepmom, but it felt like she was saying that I was not even related. Because their mother has such a difficult time with her children being with me, it's almost like they don't want to acknowledge that I'm part of the family—even after all these years."

Even with disappointments, however, hope endures. Sherry, who is both a stepmother and a stepdaughter, added, "When I see how difficult it is for my husband's children to be inclusive of me and my family, I can't help but be reminded of the tough beginning I had with my stepmother, Lucille. Today, twenty-five years later, I love Lucille as a mom and we can't live without one another. I just hope the same thing for my stepchildren one day."

In the process of accepting our limitations yet while still holding on to hope, we learn a lot about ourselves and how we relate to others. As Teresa put it, "It has made me more sensitive and understanding." Facing the challenges of stepmother-stepdaughter relationships is, among many other things, a continual learning process in which we encounter ourselves and others anew.

Encountering Ourselves and Others Anew

*"All of a sudden, I realized how much love
children need and how much more
important they are than any of my
own personal issues."*

—DIANE, STEPMOTHER, AGE 50

Being a stepmother or a stepdaughter is one of those life experiences that offers us exciting opportunities to grow personally and in relationship with one another. This growth occurs, at least partially, when we discover new things about ourselves and others, when we understand thoughts, actions, and feelings more clearly, and when we "see" people—ourselves and others—as they really are.

Prior to becoming a stepmother, Diane assumed her role would obviously not be that of "mother." Yet she said, "I had to really discover what that different role was. I must have thought it would be more of a favorite aunt or something like that. It wasn't until I was pregnant with our son and my stepdaughter was eight years old that I really got it—like an epiphany. All of a sudden, I realized how much love children need and how much more important they are than any of my own personal issues. Finally, I understood that my stepdaughter's well-being was as important as my own child's."

Sue, age fifty, also came to approach the step relationship from a place of insight like Diane's—seeing that her stepdaughter's happiness meant as much as her own child's. That perspective enabled her to see qualities in her stepdaughter, Cathleen, that she had never seen before.

"By then," Sue remembered, "Cathleen was seven and I started to see some things about her that were really wonderful. I was finally able to take a step back and really see her for the first time. Prior to that, I took really good care of her and played with her and so forth, but I didn't have my feelings sorted out about where I should be with her emotionally. Once I was a little bit older and in the position of being a parent myself, I saw there was nothing more important than the well-being of the children."

As Cathleen spoke about her stepmother, Sue, she exuded a deep warmth and said, "She was just so wonderful with me. Her approach at first was to play with me. I was this little girl and I think it made it easier for me to keep it like that. She made clothes for my doll, and I loved our time together because it was fun." As

Cathleen became older and Sue made a shift in how she chose to relate to Cathleen, their relationship naturally grew deeper and closer.

Becoming a mother herself shed new light on Louise's relationship with her stepmother, Renée. It was then that Louise began to understand how much Renée emotionally endured over the years.

"Now that I am pregnant with my third child," Louise says, "I look back and see what Renée went through with me. She was sixteen and a new mom— she'd just had her first baby. At times she would throw a fit because I was being difficult and then I would throw a fit back. We were both so young, and we could both be very immature in the way we handled things."

As we learned earlier, Karla's relationship with her stepdaughter, Melanie, was intense from the beginning. Karla didn't want or know how to include this "outsider" in her idea of the "picture-perfect" family. Her own inner struggles, eventually helped her to recognize Melanie's needs and to respond to them in a positive way.

"Although I was feeling all of this angst inside," Karla remembers, "I didn't let it show to Melanie. I just couldn't. I know she just loved the idea of having another family. When I saw that, it made me feel more tender toward her. I saw that she was just a kid and I realized how much my family and my family ethics meant to her."

Until relatively recently, however, Melanie was unaware of Karla's initial feelings toward her. Their relationship has matured over the years, allowing them to talk openly about those early years. Melanie says, "I know now how Karla felt about me, but over the years we have become very good friends. After all these years, we are closer than ever."

While Melanie very much wanted to be a part of Karla's family, Stephanie was not so sure that she wanted to have anything to do with her father's new relationship with Gloria. Stephanie's experience with a previous stepmother had been a bad one, leaving her scared, bruised, and angry with her father. She was a young adult when she met Gloria, and her first impression was that Gloria was probably just another one of "Dad's women."

Although Stephanie's father had warned Gloria that Stephanie harbored hard feelings toward her previous stepmother, he didn't tell Gloria the entire story of Stephanie's experience. At the same time, he was not communicating well with Stephanie. Because of this, Gloria carried around a false impression of the situation, which left her angry and resentful.

Gloria, however, made a wise choice, which allowed

her to approach Stephanie in a healthy and new way. Gloria decided to be neutral. She chose to be a listener and a nonjudgmental force in Stephanie's life. By behaving in manner very unlike Stephanie's previous stepmother, Gloria laid the foundation for a close relationship. Even in seemingly volatile situations, Gloria managed to become a "safe zone" for Stephanie almost from the very beginning. "I was very honest with her," Gloria said, "and I got her to open up to me in a way that she had never opened up with anybody before."

Because of her willingness to put aside her own feelings of resentment and anger, Gloria offered a safe place for Stephanie to open up and reveal who she really was and what she was feeling. This early connection allowed their relationship to deepen in the following years.

Preconceived notions, as Gloria had about Stephanie and Stephanie had about stepmothers, are major obstacles to overcome before you can accept a new stepdaughter or stepmother into your life. Not surprisingly, these preconceived notions are particularly strong when a stepdaughter discovers that her new stepmother is the woman who is partially responsible for breaking up her previously "happy" family.

The stepdaughters I interviewed who found themselves in this situation said they felt betrayed by their fathers. An extramarital affair adds another measure of tension in a divorce, a tension that affects the entire family. Although a common response may be rebellion, it's also possible that the stepdaughter may try to adjust and opt for a more positive approach. If her desire for a happy family life outweighs the inclination to stay angry, the stepdaughter may find forgiveness and a healthy relationship can be formed. Such was the case of Ariel and her stepmother, Diane.

Ariel was fourteen years old when Diane entered the picture. "My first impression of Diane," Ariel remembers, "was a little skewed because I knew the history of how they got together and how they became a couple." Ariel, now twenty-three, explains: "I had obvious issues with the effect of their relationship on my mom and dad's marriage. At the same time, I really wanted to have a normal, happy family life. Because of that, I was able to push my feelings about their affair aside. I was happy when they got married."

In the last chapter, we heard Sherry's story about becoming a stepmother to a friend's children when she married her friend's husband. Now her stepdaughter Jennifer shares her story about that time and how she moved past a very painful initial reaction to allow for a deeper, more meaningful interaction later in life.

"Sherry was a friend of my mother's," Jennifer remembered. "We spent time with her, and I really liked her—until the truth came out. Of course, I felt resentful that this woman was taking my father away. However, as I grew into my teens, I acknowledged that she was there for me like no one else ever had been."

When we openly and honestly encounter ourselves and others, our perceptions change and our eyes are opened slowly over time. We see the person who has been there all along, but in a new way. It is this capacity to see anew that allows stronger, healthier family relationships to be built. Often, as we will see in the next chapter, stepmothers are the ones who bridge family gaps and help create healthier and more intimate relationships.

Bridging Family Gaps

"Once Mary came into the picture, Dad and Mom actually started laughing, having conversations, and being much more comfortable around each other."

—STACEY, STEPDAUGHTER, AGE 32

One unexpected, and usually unacknowledged, role stepmothers often play is that of mediator and reconciler. They bridge family gaps and bring people together. Not only do they do this within the individual stepfamily unit, but they also often facilitate healthier relationships among members of the original families. Patti, for example, has helped ease tensions between the mother and father of her stepchildren.

"Mom has gone through some hard times," Patti's thirty-year-old stepdaughter, Deena, explained. "While she's always been very supportive of my sister and me, she doesn't get along with my dad. But she absolutely loves Patti! I think since Dad and Patti got together, my father has been much more relaxed with himself. Patti has guided my mom and my dad toward having better phone conversations and being more comfortable in social situations. Patti bridged that gap."

Stacey's parents were civil, but not cordial. "We've never had to deal with 'Oh, I can't invite so-and-so,'" Stacey, age thirty-two, recalled. "Mom and Dad always got along at graduations and those kinds of affairs. Even before Dad met Mary, Mom and Dad would always be decent to each other. Once Mary came into the picture, however, Dad and Mom actually started laughing, having conversations, and being much more comfortable around each other, which made the whole family thing better."

Stepmothers also facilitate relationships between daughters and mothers. "I think I have played a big part in Kelly and her mother becoming close," Susan said. One of the ways she encouraged this was to invite Kelly's mother to Thanksgiving the first year Susan and Kelly's father were married. She has continued to invite Kelly's mother to family functions ever since.

"That first Thanksgiving was very important for all of us as a family," Susan explained, "and I wanted to make sure that Kelly knew her mother was welcome. My mom and her husband were there. They were very polite and started talking to Kelly's mother right away." The seed that was planted that first year came to obvious fruition several years later. Susan explained, "It was a little uncomfortable at first, but by the time Kelly's wedding came seven years later, her mother and father were able to embrace."

Throughout the years, Gloria has been a positive force in the life of her stepdaughter, Stephanie, and the entire family. Stephanie loves the fact that her mother is welcome in their home and that she can witness her parents having conversations now after so many years of distance. "Stephanie is so thankful," Gloria says. "She really feels that I have been a catalyst in bringing the family together, and that has brought great stability to her life."

For a stepdaughter, having a stepmother who knows her dad better than anyone else is a wonderful thing in itself. A stepmother can help establish or keep a daughter-father connection alive.

"For the past couple of years," Becky, twenty-seven, commented, "I've felt that without my stepmother, Teresa, I wouldn't have had much of a relationship with my father. She initiates, she asks, she calls. Although my dad does certain things, he's not as aware as she is. If my mom and dad had stayed together, and Teresa had never been in the picture, I doubt my father and I would have developed an adult relationship. She keeps the family together. She really does."

Through their stepmothers, daughters can sometimes learn what their fathers may not be able to put into words. As Jill put it, "I discovered some of my father's deepest feelings through Sue. She would say to me, 'I know your dad doesn't tell you how proud he is of you, but I want you to know that I've heard him tell all of his friends how much you mean to him and how great he thinks you are doing.'"

Stepmothers can also protect their stepdaughters in their relationships with their fathers. "Diane was kind of the little connector between my dad and me a lot of the time," twenty-three-year-old Ariel said. "As I got older, she looked out for me, 'Don't talk to him,' she'd say. 'He's in a bad mood.'"

Diane also bridged a family gap when she divorced Lisa's father, prior to her marriage to Ariel's father. Ironically it was Diane who eventually broke the news to Lisa. "I did feel something was going on with them for a few years, though I didn't know what. Diane came to visit me in Kansas, and she and my aunt sat me down to tell me that my father and Diane were getting a divorce. I was very upset, because I didn't know how to take it. Looking at it now, it does seem interesting that Diane told me instead of my father.

"After they divorced, I think my father was very afraid that I wouldn't come to visit anymore, but almost nothing changed except that when I went to Wisconsin, I would split the time between Diane and my father." Lisa added, "Emotionally, it was never a problem; in fact, it got easier as the years went on. We would still go out as a group. I never had a problem with it because I had quality time with both."

From the beginning, Suzanne's relationship with her stepmother, Liz, had been tense. This didn't change until Suzanne, now thirty-four, was in her late teens. At a crucial moment, Liz supported her in a difficult decision—a decision Suzanne's father vehemently opposed.

"When I became pregnant at eighteen," Suzanne remembers, "my dad insisted that I put the baby up for adoption. But when my baby was born, I decided to keep him." Feeling very scared and uncertain as to how she would tell her parents, Suzanne confided in the first person to arrive at the hospital after her baby's birth— her stepmother, Liz.

"As I held my little boy," Suzanne continued, "I told Liz my decision. She took my hand and said, 'I support you 100 percent.' Then my dad came in screaming, 'You should not be holding that baby.' Liz then took *his* hand and said, 'Suzanne is keeping her child, and we must support her.' Slowly my father opened up his arms and held his little grandson for the first time. Dad started to cry—and we all cried."

Suzanne's tears came in part because Liz, whom she had shut out of her life for years, had supported her at this crucial time. Liz also helped Suzanne's father to accept Suzanne's decision and then warmly welcome his new grandchild.

Sometimes, however, stepmothers must accept that some gaps cannot be closed—for instance, dealing with the behavior of a dysfunctional parent or simply listening to a child's response to that parent. At times, the stepmother must put her personal opinions about the biological parent aside in hopes of providing the child with a happier, healthier environment.

"Rhonda will come home and be hysterical for two hours because she can't believe her mother is doing something," Kathy said. "We point out that there are certain things you have to accept about people. 'This is how your mom is and she loves you,' we tell her. There are certain things I would love to say, but I always ask myself, 'Is it fair to Rhonda to say that?'"

In the efforts to bring families and family members together, it can be important to invite mothers and the extended family to special events, even if they choose not to accept. For children, having the whole family together makes a difference, even if it is only for a few hours. Children like to feel that extra love and support.

Jill, a twenty-three-year-old stepdaughter, remembers family outings as fun, joyous events. They meant having all the people she loves together in one place.

"The most joyous events were those that included everyone I love," Jill said. "Seven of my best girlfriends graduated from high school with me. Five of them have divorced parents, and have remarried at least once or twice. We had a party in the park and invited everyone. All the parents and all the steps showed up. It lasted the whole night long and we had a great time."

Caroline recalls, "I have always tried to include my stepdaughter's mom in important events in Ashley's life. Sometimes she makes it, sometimes she doesn't. But I always try, because it's important to the kids. When Ashley graduated from sixth grade, I called up her mom and her mother's mother and invited them. Ashley's mom and I have always gotten along fine. There's obviously a little bit of tension, but I've always encouraged her to be a part of things."

Holidays pose a particular challenge in combined households, but they also offer an opportunity to come together as extended families. Ariel recalls the difficulties of Christmas apart. "I was so young when they got divorced, that I never really had my mother and father together. Now it's something very special when I see them together. "One year, my stepmother, Diane, invited my mother for Christmas dinner because she felt bad that we never all celebrated together. I always had to get up on Christmas morning to go to a different house. It's great when we have everyone we love together, and nice not feeling like a yo-yo."

Lisa, Diane's first stepdaughter, also remembers the challenge of Christmas. Before her father and Diane divorced, her holiday was split between her stepdad and mom and her father and Diane. "I would have Christmas at home with my mom and my stepdad," Lisa recalls, "and then I would fly to see my dad and Diane after Christmas. I would have two Christmases. The tree was still set up at Dad and Diane's, and they would save some presents for Jamie, Diane's son, to open. Diane would also always buy presents for Jeremie, my brother, as well as for my mother and stepdad. My mother also would buy presents for Diane. The two families never spent anytime together, but gifts symbolized the efforts to maintain a healthy connection."

Weddings, too, can be a time of bridging gaps. Susan, reflecting on her stepdaughter's wedding, said, "Their mother has played a very important role in the children's lives over the years. From a difficult start to a functioning co-family, everyone benefits when the families can come together. When there's a special event, I always say, what is it to take five or six hours to be with your husband's ex or my ex? I know how good it makes Kelly feel when she sees all of us together. That's all that matters during those special times."

This sentiment places the emotional ties of the combined and extended families in the forefront. Stepmothers' efforts to bridge the gaps within their own combined families as well as with extended families are acts of love and commitment to the health and wholeness of the families of which they are all a part.

Daring

Creating New Ways
of Being Family

We don't usually think of family life as being a daring activity, but it is. Choosing to be a family—with all of its challenges and pain as well as its opportunities and joys—takes courage, a word that is rooted in the French and Latin words for "heart." And that's what is takes to be a family—a lot of heart.

Choosing to be a combined family means entering the unknown of new relationships. In the past, this "unknown" had few healthy models. Today good models are more common as the number of combined families' increases. But the challenge remains as these families seek—and dare—to create new ways of being family, which necessitates family members discovering who they really are.

This discovery allows them to move more authentically and freely into relationship so that a new family can be birthed. Like the birth of a child, this usually involves labor, pain, and joy. When a child, or a family, is conceived, we don't know what it will be like, yet when it is born, it is greeted with wonder and joy.

Daring to create new ways of being family means enabling mothers, stepmothers, and stepdaughters to interact and grow with one another. No one exists in isolation from others, and the women who compose this special threesome must deepen, strengthen, and push the edges of their relationships. As a result, they grow both individually and together.

Perhaps one of the most daring, heart-filled ways of being family is also the most simple: being there for those we love. By being there, we bring comfort, give support, offer advice, and simply show how much we care.

The stories in this section tell of people pushing themselves as they develop into a family. Stepmothers and stepdaughters share how they discovered who they really are; what was involved in birthing a new family; how they grew as stepmothers, stepdaughters, and mothers; and finally how they were there for those they love—a sure sign of the health and vitality of these combined families.

Discovering Who We Are

"You are like the mother without being the mother. It can be very confusing."

—DIANE, STEPMOTHER, AGE 50

The changes inherent with the combining of families seem to invite questions like "Who am I?" or "Who am I now that I'm in this new relationship?" Stepmothers may have questions about their role, such as "Am I a mother, or not?" and "Just what exactly is a stepmother supposed to do, or not do?" Stepdaughters often have similar questions: "Am I her daughter?" or "What exactly is a stepdaughter?" These basic questions are important in and of themselves, but they also open the door to discovering a deeper understanding of oneself, others, and what is truly important in life.

It may sound simplistic, but we discover who we are when we pose the question to ourselves—and then have the courage to find the answer. Sometimes it takes a while for the response to come. Sometimes it comes only after "trying on" different answers. For example, stepmothers, when they are unsure of how to define their role, may try on being friends or older "sisters" with their stepdaughters. But being a friend or an older sister doesn't quite ring true, because there are other unique dimensions to the stepmother-stepdaughter relationship. Discovering those dimensions, and the particular form of stepmotherhood in one's own relationship, can take time. Often the process begins with simply not having a clue about how to proceed.

"I was completely unprepared for what my role should be when I became a stepmother," Sue, now fifty, confesses. "In 1974, there were hardly any books on stepparenting, and I didn't know anyone who was even a parent, let alone a stepparent. My stepdaughter, Cathleen, would come to visit us four times a year. I took care of her, but I felt awkward because she wasn't mine. I had this fantasy of what it would be like—that it would be easy and I would be just like her mom. I don't even know where that came from. I did anything to feel more involved in her life. It helped me a lot, but the whole picture didn't become clear until many years later."

This time of soul searching can leave a stepmother feeling very alone and isolated. If her husband is either unable or unwilling to support her, for whatever reason—lack of communication skills, busy work schedule, business travel, and so on—her insecure feelings may increase.

"My husband at the time wasn't a very communicative person," Diane said, "so I didn't have the opportunity to talk through my feelings about this with him. I felt quite alone. I remember being easily upset and jealous. I was jealous of his previous relationship, which his daughter represented. And I don't think he had completely worked through the loss of his first marriage, so that just added to my insecurities. Through it all, I still wanted to develop a relationship with my stepdaughter, but I knew I had to figure out what my role was. I also had to do it alone. I determined after much reflection that I wasn't a mother to her and I didn't have to be, but what did that make me? I was still confused as to who I was in this relationship."

Lisa, Diane's stepdaughter, didn't live with Diane and her husband, which may have added to Diane's quandary. And because Lisa lived with her mother and stepfather in another state, she didn't see her dad and Diane regularly. Lisa's visits were more like a yearly getaway from her mother and stepfather. Diane's house was always a good place for Lisa to visit, because Diane made it fun and exciting.

"Once when we were going on one of our yearly excursions," Lisa remembered, "I asked Dad and Diane why I had two dads. That was very interesting because I never asked why I had two mothers. When I was young, I never thought about Diane as a mother figure. She was very young, much younger than my biological mother, and she did things with me that my mom never did. She was more like an older sister to me and definitely a fun person to play with."

Lisa, now twenty-nine, can't believe that Diane was only twenty-four when she was doing all of this. "I think—twenty-four years old. How would I be raising a four-year-old? I wouldn't know how to handle it. I think the decisions and choices she made were amazing, especially for her age."

Lisa, in retrospect, understands things about her relationship with her stepmother that she was unaware of at the time. In reflecting on that, she also discovers something about herself—that she can't imagine being twenty-four and raising a four-year-old. What we have learned about ourselves in the past helps us deal with the present. For Diane, that meant when she became a stepmother for the second time (in her second marriage), she discovered who she was—or wasn't—in that relationship.

"Because I was involved in every facet of Ariel's life, it was easy to start feeling that I was her mother," Diane said. "You can get pretty hurt when you realize that you're really not this child's mother, but understanding that is a big piece of being a stepmother: you are like the mother without being the mother. It can be very confusing. With Ariel I learned another thing: now I *was* a mother. I had a son, Jamie. At first I tried to treat them equally. Then I realized that Ariel had this additional mother-person. I realized that I had to be primary mother to Jamie and that I wasn't going to have the same relationship with Ariel that I had with my son. We were all more comfortable with being who we really were. My son needed me as his primary mother, just like Ariel needed to have her own mother."

As stepmothers like Sue and Diane seek to discover who they are and how they can best be stepmothers, they may consciously or unconsciously also help their stepdaughters toward self-awareness. Lynda, a fifty-three-year-old stepmother, keeps a card from her stepdaughter, Beth, sitting on her desk. When I interviewed her, she was in the process of moving, but the card remained in its place.

"Beth sent me flowers with this card," Lynda explained. "The card says, 'Dear Mom, Thank you for helping me be who I am. Happy Mother's Day. Love, Beth.' Then she wrote a letter to me explaining that if it hadn't been for me, she wasn't sure what would have happened to her. She also said how much I've helped her be who she is."

Like many stepmothers and stepdaughters, Lynda

and Beth have learned a lot from each other. Their lives exemplify that only by giving do you see and learn so much about yourself.

Learning about oneself isn't always an easy process, even if it ultimately is a good one. Erika, now twenty-three, needed to learn to be her own age. Most of her early childhood was spent with her mother. Erika recalls, "Because of my mom's inability to be a mother, to be an adult, I grew up very quickly. The good side of that is I learned how to be responsible. The bad side is I always expected to be able to call all the shots."

When Erika moved in with her father and step-mother, Joanna, the situation changed drastically. She remembers, "I was thirteen going on thirty. Though it was really hard and we had lots of fights about this, I eventually got to be a kid. For the first time in my life, I got to be who I really was."

Erika's father and stepmother helped her find who she really was—and what age she really was. In doing that, they also helped her discover what she wanted for herself. Ironically, stepchildren may even help a step-mother recognize what she desires for her own biological child. When Carol, now forty-one, was in her twenties and pregnant with her own son, she saw her stepdaughter, Lindsey, as a reminder of what she hoped to have with her own child one day. Carol recalls, "I saw that my stepdaughter had some wonderful qualities that I hadn't really seen before. One prime example was her initiative. We went out for lunch once when she was just a little girl. She wanted ketchup, so she went right up to the counter and asked the man for it. I noticed how poised and independent she was. As I was looking at her, I thought, I want my child to be able to do that. That's so wonderful. It made me think about helping a child become independent and confident."

Stepchildren may also help us see who we've been—and how we might want to change that. Sherry, who was a stepdaughter before she became a stepmother, remembers, "Every Christmas my stepmother, Lucille, had a huge Christmas gathering, and I would always be late. I figured I would go after I was done with my own Christmas celebration. I wasn't responsible or mature, and I now see how much effort she put into it. Dinner for fifty people would not be served because I wasn't there yet."

It has been Sherry's experience as a stepmother that has helped her see this behavior in a new way. Faced with the ongoing obstacles of being a stepmother, she has had to come to terms with a lot of things about herself. Through her own stepchildren's actions, she sees Lucille in a new light. She knows now how hard a stepmother can work over a long period of time to better a situation, but still not get a return on her investment. "I remember Lucille would want to discuss difficult things about my dad, but I just basically blew them off," Sherry said. "I did not realize how important her attempts were until I became a stepmother."

In the past six or seven years, Sherry and Lucille have become very close, at least partially because of Sherry's growing self-awareness. "When I finally became a stepmother myself," Sherry explained, "I realized all that Lucille had tried to do over the years."

Discovering who we are—and who others are as well—can change our perceptions. Some of my interviewees told me that their perceptions of "family" have changed drastically since being part of a combined family. "Family" has acquired an entirely fresh meaning. Sometimes we learn this the hard way, as Karla did when her marriage failed.

As her nineteen-year marriage disintegrated, Karla began examining everything around her. She wanted to figure out what people really meant to her. She started reevaluating her family. She thought that things would stay the same forever, but, as Karla put it, "it was falling apart all around me. I had to ask myself, 'What is family? What is it, *really*?' My stepdaughter, Melanie, is very different from my own children. I realized that I had been resenting her all these years because she threatened my picture of the ideal family. When that family crumbled, I realized that families are what you make them. Families are the people that you give your love to and include in your life. At some point I realized that I could really enrich Melanie's life, and I could let her enrich mine as well. I realized that she didn't have to be exactly like my kids in order to have my love and be a part of my family."

Though difficult, loss can sometimes help us accept others—and ourselves. Relationships allow us to discover who we really are and who we want to become. As Caroline remarked about having stepchildren, "It's made me a better person, so that when I had my own children I was a more loving, selfless person." Acceptance is an important and helpful quality to have as one seeks to birth a new family.

Birthing a New Family

*"I learned that family . . . has to do
with really caring about someone, and not
so much about them being your own flesh
and blood."*

—CAROL, STEPMOTHER, AGE 41

One issue that arises early in stepfamilies is that of naming or identity. What terms do we use to identify one another? What implications are there for those terms? For some families, the issue is not that important. For others, it is. Sometimes, as it was for Louise, it is a critical issue for one family member.

Louise, a thirty-one-year-old stepdaughter, never liked the term "half brother" or "half sister." For her, it represented a division of her family. Louise remembers, "One day Felice, my seven-year-old half sister, came to me and said, 'You're my half sister, right?' And I said, 'Half sister? Who told you that?' It turned out someone at school had told her. It really bothered me, so I told her, 'If anyone ever asks you if I am your sister, what do you say? Am I your sister or your half sister?' She looked at me and said quietly, 'You're my sister.'

92

'Right,' I responded, 'and don't pay attention to what people say.'

"Felice *is* my sister," Louise explained. "I have always felt that my stepbrothers and stepsisters are a huge part of me; nothing separates us. We are 100 percent siblings. We are so close, so much a part of each other, that there is no way we aren't just plain brothers and sisters."

Some adults also have difficulties with the usual labels for members of combined families. Margaret, a fifty-three-year-old stepmother, did not respond well to the "step" label and made the choice very early on to eliminate it from her relationship with Debbie. "I would never use the word 'stepdaughter' to refer to her," Margaret said. "I have always called her my daughter, I've always thought of her as my daughter. I didn't want to make it seem like we were separate in any way."

Naming implies defining, and for Carol, a forty-one-year-old stepmother, the experience of living in a combined family completely changed her thinking about what "family" was. "I learned that family is a broader term than just your own immediate family," Carol said. "It has to do with really caring about someone, and not so much about them being your own flesh and blood."

The experience of creating a new family involves a lot of this caring—whether it be for people who are related to you biologically or emotionally through marriage. Much of a family's attention is directed toward children, as stepparents and parents seek to do what is best, or most important, for their children and stepchildren alike.

In my own case, I am certain that my parents—all of them—discussed how this transition into a newly combined family would affect me. Time and effort must have been taken for them to work out all the little details that made up my life. It was not always an easy time for me, but their care and concern helped moving into this new family reality go as smoothly as could be expected.

The development of a new family, however, goes on beyond just the transition time. It takes place in the common, everyday things that make up a life together. For a stepmother who takes over day-to-day "mom" responsibilities, this involves teaching her stepdaughter about life; providing stability and security (especially if the stepdaughter's experience with her mother or previous stepmother has been difficult or painful); being a role model; and last, but of course not least, loving and caring for her stepdaughter in countless ways.

Some stepmothers give their stepdaughters a new chance at life and loving relationships. "I put Beth under my wing and gave her her childhood back,"

Lynda said. "When she left her mother at the age of twelve and came to live with us, my approach was to be loving and kind and understanding. What she ultimately wanted was for her mother to be me, but, of course, that wasn't possible. What *was* possible was that I became like a mother to her. During that year when she decided to live with us, I asked her what she wanted to call me, Lynda or Mom. She said, 'Mom.' Sure enough the first day, she came home from school, she said, 'Mom, I'm home!' It was like an epiphany: in our own way, we *were* mother and daughter."

A major responsibility most stepmothers are eager to fill is offering their stepdaughters emotional and practical help. Sometimes those two combine, as in Kathy's case.

"When Rhonda was in fifth grade," Kathy, twenty-nine, explained, "I took her out to buy tampons and pads. She didn't have her period yet, but I got her the things she would need and said, 'Look, this is a really personal time for a girl. You might be embarrassed and might not want to tell anybody about it, so I'm going make sure you have everything you need. If you want to talk with me about it, you can. If you want to talk to your mom about it, you can. Here's what you'll need. Here's how to use it.' This helped her feel comfortable talking to me about it. The day that she actually got her period, she told me and she stayed home from school, and it was fine."

The special advantage that stepmothers have in giving emotional or psychological support is rarely acknowledged or recognized.

"I think our biggest breakthrough was when Faith was in college," Lesley, a forty-nine-year-old stepmother, said. "She had a difficult time. I think what I could offer Faith, more than anyone else in her life, was my ability to be more objective about her. I feel that I really know her strengths. With your own child you tend to get more shaken up when they're having problems. Since I'm not her parent, I can see things more objectively. I can truly tell her anything and know that she'll be okay."

That special kind of objectivity, joined with deep caring, is particularly helpful in situations where stepmothers must take the place of an absent mother, and reassure the children that she will be there for them, as was the case for Caroline. Because of their mother's inability to care for her children, the courts gave Caroline's husband full custody. When Caroline came into their lives, at twenty years old, she chose to make these children a priority.

"We try to make sure the kids feel support and love," Caroline explained. "Especially now that they're older, I don't want them to walk on eggshells around me. Yes, I want them to care about my feelings as much as I care about theirs, but I don't want them to be afraid or apprehensive because they know I'm not their biological mom. If their own biological mom could leave, they think a stepmother certainly could leave too."

As Caroline worked to fill some of her stepchildren's emotional gaps, she also took on some of the practical holes in her stepdaughter's life. "I just wanted to do things with Ashley that her mother hadn't taken an interest in. I took her shopping, did her hair—fun things. I planned her seventh birthday party, which was the first birthday that I spent with Ashley and her father. We put together this huge slumber party with thirteen of her girlfriends. I didn't get in there as a disciplinarian; I got in there as somebody who loved them and just liked to have fun. I wanted to spend time with them."

Holidays, of course, are also a part of the creation of a new family. New traditions are born, and old ones are incorporated in fresh ways. This is done within the constraints and possibilities presented by the combining of families. For parents and stepchildren alike, understanding and compromise go into making holidays beautiful and positive experiences.

I always had Christmas Eve with my mom and Christmas with my dad. Before my dad married Linda,

Dad and I would gather around a rubber tree plant, which we'd decorated with red and blue balls hanging on its puny leaves. When my stepmother, Linda, came into our lives, that was the last we ever saw of the rubber tree—at least as a Christmas tree. Now we had a real Christmas tree.

When Dad and Linda moved into a larger house, another tradition was born. We—Dad, Linda, my half brother John, and me—would go to a Christmas tree farm and cut a tree we liked. While I remember fondly the days of the rubber tree plant with the blue and red balls and all the presents leaning up against the planter, my brother never knew that tradition. New traditions have replaced old ones.

Stepmothers sometimes play an instrumental role in creating memorable traditions for stepchildren who have not had them before. "Christmas was never a big deal at Janeen's house," Cynthia said. "She's learned all she knows about family holidays from me. When Christmastime came around, I made sure that Janeen had just as many gifts as my own kids did. In fact, I went to great pains to make sure she would feel the same as everyone else."

Extra efforts made for special events create happy memories, especially when family members lay aside differences for the sake of the children.

Jill, a twenty-three-year-old stepdaughter, finds satisfaction in making people happy; it is difficult for her when people are unhappy. As an emotionally observant person, she realizes that her mother has mixed feelings about her stepmother, and that her father harbors feelings of guilt. "I know all these feelings exist," Jill says, "but when we're able to put them aside and celebrate a happy event, those are the best times for me."

Beyond special events, stepmothers also find ways every day to do what is best for their stepdaughters—helping them grow, build their confidence, and become themselves.

"My acceptance of Tiffany is one of our strengths," Judith, age forty-four, explained. "Acceptance is a very important part of our relationship. I tell her I love her all the time. I tell her she is fabulous. I try to make her feel special about herself. I think I may be the only person in her life who makes her feel really, really special. I am always telling her how proud I am of her and how great I think she is doing."

Supporting a child doesn't stop when a child is no longer a child. Monica was a young woman when her father married her stepmother, Leah. This relationship has given Monica a sense of stability that she didn't have before.

"I have finally seen my father have a relationship with

a woman," Monica said. She went on to explain how difficult it was having a father who was single and the "man about town." Her parents never married, so she hadn't ever seen her dad as a father or as a husband until Leah came into their lives. "I never knew if I could count on him," Monica commented. "After he married Leah, I was able to respect him more. I now have a sense of home. I am able to spend time with him, like I never could before. Because of Leah, he has finally grown up. He is able to emote so much more now, and he is able to tell me how much he loves me, which I needed to hear. Leah has been the catalyst for this new, complete relationship.

Despite stepmothers' efforts to do what they can for their stepdaughters, the birthing of a family doesn't always go smoothly. Pamela, a thirty-seven-year-old stepdaughter and stepmother, left home when she was eighteen. In an effort to maintain her own identity, she ran from a household that had a lot of difficulties. "I was very judgmental of my dad," Pamela said. "I just wanted to take care of myself as much as I could. We had a super-ficial, kind of fun relationship. He had his problems and I had mine. He didn't interfere with my problems and I never interfered in his. When Marjorie, my stepmother, came into the relationship, she wanted to talk about some of the difficulties, but I'd just blow her off."

Marjorie remembers trying to speak with Pamela many years ago about her concern that Pamela's father might have a drinking problem. Pamela's response, Marjorie recalls, was "If that's going to bother you, that's just too bad." Marjorie now says, "I realized then that you don't go around saying things like that to your husband's daughter; you're interfering with the father-daughter relationship. But it really hurt me, and years later I told Pamela that."

Fortunately for Pamela and Marjorie, their relationship grew past that tense time. Pamela now says, "When she told me that my reluctance to talk about important things really hurt her feelings, that's when I thought about how my stepchildren treat me. I realized then how difficult it must have been all those years for Marjorie. It's rather strange to look back at it, because I value her friendship so much now."

Over time, Pamela's relationship with Marjorie underwent a transformation. Frequently, it seems, such developments are part of the process a new family experiences. Gloria's stepdaughter, Stephanie, experienced a particularly interesting transformation, simply because Gloria's daughter Donna looked up to Stephanie.

Though Stephanie's teenage years were troubled, she ended up becoming a role model for Donna. Gloria says, "Donna placed Stephanie on a pedestal. She adored Stephanie right off the bat. In turn, Stephanie was, and is, extremely protective of Donna. Because of that, Stephanie didn't want Donna to know about the things she was doing—risky behavior like drugs and so on. She literally put herself on check for Donna's sake—to protect her. Then when Donna went through her own problems in her late teens with drugs, Stephanie would go crazy. She had really changed."

Though not all of Stephanie's risky behavior had changed, she had grown beyond a lot of it. This became clear when she discovered that she was pregnant. Gloria explains, "She looked at me and said, 'I am going to have to change my life.' Together we went down the list of the positive things she had done. I didn't want to beat the negative into her. She had had enough of that. With a lot of love from her father and me, Stephanie turned her life around."

Like Gloria, Margaret, age fifty-three, looks back in wonder at the transformation that occurred in her step-daughter's life, especially given how their relationship started. "Debbie did not like me, because I was another woman in her father's life. Over a period of time—and through me choosing to become a mother figure to her—our relationship grew. The first concrete sign of this transformation came when she was twelve and she stayed with us for the summer. Prior to coming out, she called us and said that she only needed a one-way ticket. She told me she was not going back and she didn't want me to tell her mother. A week before she was supposed to go home, we called her mother and Debbie told her that she wanted to stay with us. Her mother was very upset, but Debbie was determined and remained very strong throughout the conversation. We stood by her. She never went back. It took courage for her to choose a situation that would be better for her."

The transformations don't only happen for children. In speaking about her relationships with her stepdaughters, Diane said, "Being a stepmother has helped me grow up and realize how important children are. They've taught me how to not be selfish. Realizing what was really important helped me be a better parent to my son. I was able to let things go that weren't important and remember that kids are not just moldable people—that they have their own strengths, their own personalities."

As the birthing of a new family occurs, it is not surprising that stepmothers and stepdaughters reflect on and come to a new appreciation of the meaning of family. Teresa smiles and says, "My husband and I value everyone in our family, no matter where they come from and who they are. In our family, everyone counts." Stacey credits her stepmother, Mary, with helping her "realize how important family is." And Kathy realizes that no one individual is responsible for the creation of a new family: "I don't take all the credit nor would I give all the credit to my husband. It's all of us working together for the betterment of our family."

For a family to thrive, all parties must work together, but a very special working relationship exists among moms, stepmoms, and stepdaughters, as we will see in the next chapter.

Growing Together:
Moms, Stepmoms, and Stepdaughters

*"I've learned that a family includes the
people you love and welcome into your life,
whether they be love or birth relations."*

—Karla, STEPMOTHER, AGE 39

There are many variations on the theme of moms, step-moms, and stepdaughters. Some relationships are a three-way blessing; others are a curse. Some begin in hesitance and suspicion, but end in polite connection. Others may be civil yet cool, or warm and amiable. Whatever form they take, these relationships are often at the crux of a combined family. Mothers and stepmothers almost always are strong influences on their daughters and stepdaughters, and vice versa. Together they offer each other great opportunities for growth, whether that be through positive or negative experiences.

I have had the incredible experience of having two very different yet major influences in my life—my mother, Ann, and my stepmother, Linda. They both have given me so much, and our relationships have been completely positive forces in my life. I consider myself fortunate. I know that my life would have been entirely different had I not had my mother and my stepmother striving to create a healthy and happy family experience for me.

My mother and stepmother met for the first time when Linda and my dad were picking me up one day to spend the weekend with them. Normally, Linda stayed in the car while my father ran in to get me, but this particular Saturday was different. Linda remembers it this way: "Karen ran out to the car to tell me that her dog, Sassy, just had puppies. She wanted me to come in and see them. I was introduced to Ann, and then we all sat on the floor cuddling with the new squirmy bundles of fur. Ann was trying to talk me into adopting one. I kept resisting. Our bantering was very light and playful, but it set the tone of what was to become a casual yet mutually respectful relationship over many years. Her daughter was spending two days out of every week in my company, and it was obviously in both our best interests to keep lines of communication open."

One of the greatest gifts Linda and my mother gave me, besides their unconditional love, was the opportunity to love them both. I didn't have to choose between them. Also, because they are quite different women, I was able to experience, contemplate, and enjoy their different perspectives, approaches to life, and ways of being. I grew because they offered me so much of their unique and wonderful selves.

That can be one of the true gifts of combined families—the opportunities for girls, young women, and even adult women to have mothers and stepmothers of different styles and personalities enrich their lives. Sometimes, as they were in Ariel's life, the contrasts between moms and stepmoms are surprising.

"My mom," Ariel confesses, "was my best friend. She was so fun and crazy and wild. We had the best time together. Diane, my stepmom, was more like the typical mom: 'Put your hat on. Put your coat on. Take care of yourself. You're burning the candle at both ends.' That was her main way with me."

Stepdaughters usually relate somewhat differently to their mothers than they do to their stepmothers. Each woman—the stepdaughter included—offers something different. Amy, Mary's stepdaughter, explained, "I get different things from different relationships. On a very deep level, I'm completely fulfilled with my dear friends and my biological mother. It's not that I wouldn't go to those depths with Mary, but it's just that we never have had to explore that. Perhaps that's something that we can work on together. I know if we ever were in a deep conversation, I would be able to be totally open with her. There's just lightness about Mary. I love how humorous she is. It's a beautiful quality. I always see her light and acknowledge it."

Sometimes it takes a stepdaughter a while to recognize the good qualities of her stepmother. Though it has taken time, Becky has learned to love and admire her stepmother, Teresa. "I've known Teresa for more than half my life," Becky said. "My mother and Teresa are two very different women. But they're both hard working, and they both love their families and would do anything for them. In their own ways, they have both shown me how to care about people. They've been able to show me a lot of variety and have been influential in raising me. Although I didn't spend a lot of time with Teresa, she's never been the yelling-and-screaming type that my mother could be. She's given me silent support, where my mother has been more verbal. When I stand back and really see them, I realize that each was able to support me in her own way. Though it was very hard at first, having a stepmother has been a positive experience in my life."

Suzanne, thirty-four, refused to recognize her stepmother's good qualities for many years. This quickly changed when Suzanne, at eighteen, had a baby. Although her father wanted her to give the baby up for adoption, Liz sided with Suzanne in her decision to keep her baby, As the whole family grew to accept

Suzanne's little son, they also grew to accept each other. Suzanne said, "My stepmother and mother became good friends, and we all became closer than ever. Holidays are now a time for the entire family to get together and give thanks. The pettiness that once was there is now gone, and I feel I have a real family for the first time in my life."

The whole family benefits when moms and step-moms can work together as my mom and Linda have done. Linda has always credited many aspects of her successful marriage and her relationship with me to the amazing support and rapport she has had with my mother.

Although some mothers and stepmothers relate only at a distance, others literally work together for the good of their child. I mentioned in the preface how my step-mother and mother cared for me after I was badly injured by a hit-and-run driver. Watching them together as they took care of me made my healing process that much easier. I felt doubly fortunate to have both of them in my life.

Due to the severity of my injury—a compound open fracture—I had to have frequent bandage changes. Mom and Linda developed a system: one day Mom would change the nauseating bandages and Linda would change them the next. The only problem was,

Mom always passed out at the sight of blood. I would then try to do it myself, but then Linda would try to help, and my Mom too—when she came to. We ended up laughing hysterically. Maybe that laughter, shared with the two women I love most in the world, was just as important to my healing as the clean bandages were.

Just as the hardship of my injury brought my mother and stepmother together in a deeper way, moms and stepmoms can also come together through beautiful moments. This was the case for Stephanie's mother and her stepmother, Gloria.

"When Stephanie had her baby," Gloria remembered, "she included me in the room with her mother. I never got the sense from her that she felt the need to divide her time between her 'mom' and her 'stepmom.' She introduced us to the woman who shared her hospital room by saying, 'These are my moms.' After the baby was born, Stephanie's mom and I were both just sobbing and holding hands. We were celebrating this beautiful day and remembering the more difficult times when it seemed like this would never be possible. Stephanie's mother then leaned her head on my shoulder as if to say, 'Oh, my God, Gloria—I am so glad you're here. We did it.'"

The connection between a stepmother and mother can even bring comfort to a stepdaughter after her mother's death. Because she had been friends with her stepchildren's mother, Pat was able to share a bit about that important friendship with her stepdaughter, Joan, at Joan's brother's wedding.

"The wedding had gone beautifully," Pat remembered. "Joan and I were sitting on a bench during the reception. When she became extremely sentimental and told me how sad it made her that her mother was not able to see her son get married before she died. Joan opened up with me, and we both cried. Her mother and I had been great friends, so as I held Joan I told her, "I know what you mean. Your mother was a very special person and always a good friend to me.' At that moment, I felt like we were meeting soul to soul. We were really talking from our hearts."

Such connections sometimes come at unexpected times and in unexpected places, especially when mothers and stepmothers are involved. This happened in my own life between my mom and my stepmom, Linda.

"After about three years of dating, John and I came to a crossroads in our relationship," Linda remembers. "We decided not to see each other anymore. Of course it also meant that I wouldn't be seeing Karen either. The separation lasted two and a half months. The first week we were back together, I took the usual Saturday morning ride with him to pick up Karen. John told me later that as he came out the front door, Ann said to him in half-jest, 'I see Linda's back. Don't blow it this time.' We were married two months later."

When a mother supports a stepmother the situations aren't always as light as those between Linda and my mom. After separating from her husband, Diane received unexpected support from her stepdaughter's mother. As mentioned earlier, Diane had to tell Lisa about the separation. Lisa's mother didn't know about the separation either, so Diane took on that task as well.

"I called Lisa's mother to break the news, and she really opened up to me. 'You know,' she said, 'I really appreciate what you're going through. I know where you are and I support you.' She then thanked me for taking such good care of Lisa and reminded me that if I hadn't encouraged the relationship, Lisa and her father very well might not have continued to interact. That was so kind of her to say. Although I haven't spoken to her much since then, it was great to have my stepdaughter's mother acknowledge me."

The times of good connection between mothers and stepmothers are often balanced by times of challenge. These times require a great deal of diplomacy. Though her parents' relationship is going better now, Faith remembers a time when diplomacy and civility played an important role in keeping a special day special.

"It's fun now that everything has kind of settled down and I can see my parents together," Faith, a twenty-three-year-old stepdaughter, explained. "They actually have a good time. But it can be uncomfortable sometimes. Once there was a surprise party for me. My dad and Lesley, my stepmother, were invited. My mom brought me to the party, and when we walked in, I thought, 'Oh boy, we're all going to be together!' Then one of my friends came up to me and said, 'What's going to happen? Are they going to fight?' Lesley was in the corner alone and my dad was partying with all my friends. My mom walked over to my stepmom and said, 'Lesley, would you like to sit down and talk?' They had a nice chat and as I watched, I felt so relieved. I felt my mom was the best mom in the entire world for doing that. It was awesome that they could put aside their stuff, show they could be mature, and move into a good relationship with each other."

Caroline also remembers an incident with her step-daughter's mother that could have turned out worse than it did. "At that time, Mark and I weren't getting along very well with Ashley's mother. Ashley was really concerned. She wanted us all to go to her seventh grade back-to-school night, a really important event for her. Before she went, she said to me, 'I'm sorry my mom makes you uncomfortable, but I still hope you'll come.'

She wanted us both there. At first I said, 'No, I'm not going, Ashley.' Then I realized that was selfish. Her mother's behavior wasn't Ashley's fault and I needed to be the adult here. So I went.

"I did most of the talking to the teachers," Caroline continued. "Ashley's mom ended up leaving early. Ashley was okay with that, but she showed concern about both of our feelings all evening. I felt really horrible that she had to be in that position."

Special events can, and often do, raise tensions for mothers and stepmothers. The challenge for stepmothers is to remain diplomatic. Weddings seem to stir up tensions like no other event.

"When she was planning her wedding, Tiffany announced to me that she wanted me to be escorted down the aisle after her mother," Judith, age forty-four, remembers. "I told her that I didn't feel comfortable with it because this was her mother's day. I think you only have one mother who brings you through her body, and she is the one who should be honored. Tiffany freaked out because she felt that I was just as much a mother to her as her own mother. She felt it would be dishonoring me if she didn't show everybody in that church how she felt about me. I respected her wishes and did what I felt was the right thing to do: I called her mother.

"'Tiffany is determined that I should walk down the aisle,' I said to her. 'I just want to see how you feel about it.' Her mother was fine with it. She told me that it was Tiffany's wedding, and whatever she wanted to do was fine with her. The wedding was beautiful—and," Judith added with a smile, "I did walk down the aisle."

As close as some stepmothers are to their stepdaughters, when occasions like weddings come up, they try as much as possible to remain neutral. True emotions of love and joy, however, cannot always be defined by roles. Because of this, wedding preparations can bring up some very complicated issues between stepmothers and mothers.

Mary and her husband's ex-wife were often friendly—until her stepdaughter Stacey's wedding. "I thought everyone got along until the wedding invitations were to be printed," Mary recalled. "Stacey's mother was very threatened by the idea of my name being on the invitation." Wanting to respect her mother's wishes, Stacey phoned Mary and gently discussed the situation. I said, "'That's okay, no one reads those things anyway.'"

Stacey knew that this was very painful for Mary. So on the day of the wedding, she walked down the aisle and gave roses to her mother, stepmother, and mother-in-law. Mary knew that she was receiving this rose as symbol of acceptance and love. Though usually not an outwardly emotional person, Mary found herself crying because she felt acknowledged for her role in the family.

The situation with Mary's second stepdaughter, Amy, will be different. "Amy is getting married at our house. The last time I let it slide, but this time, I'm putting my foot down, especially since it's at my house." Mary knew Amy's mother might not approve, so it was Amy's turn to call her mother and explain.

Amy relates her conversation with her mother: "I said, 'Mom, because we're having my wedding at Dad and Mary's house, I need to have Mary's name included. Mary never said anything, but I think it was very hard for her not to be included on Stacey's invitation. And because she's not the wicked stepmother, because she didn't break up your marriage, and because she's been a really good influence, there's no reason not to have her included and recognized as my dad's wife.' I knew it was a very touchy situation, but you know what's interesting? As soon as I presented it this way, my mom totally backed off and gave me her blessing, which was cool." This made all the difference for Mary, who at that moment felt accepted and appreciated as a part of the family.

Marie, a fifty-seven-year-old stepmother, experienced a similar feeling of acceptance and appreciation, but only after some painful adjustments were made. When Marie's older stepdaughter, Judy, came to her and said she was getting married, they discussed having Marie make her a beautiful wedding dress. Judy's mother and aunt, however, made a big deal about the making of the dress. Finally Marie decided it would be best if Judy just bought the dress. This was a very painful experience for her, and it took months for her to feel included again. "I knew this was her mother and father's day," Marie explained, "and that I should stay out of it."

Marie, however, had a promise to keep. "I had promised to make Judy the keepsake garter that you pass on to your daughter, so I did," Marie said. "I sent it to her as a surprise at her wedding shower. She loved it. Now she has asked me to do more and more things for the wedding. Beyond being acknowledged for the work I am capable of doing, I am just so happy to help."

Stepmothers know situations like weddings can be very sensitive for the mother and need to be handled with care. Diplomacy goes a long way in creating a better extended family relationship. Hopefully, too, it will lead to more positive relationships among mothers, stepmothers, and stepdaughters.

There are many ways in which this special threesome can grow, and it is especially wonderful when those involved can grow together instead of apart. For some, like Stacey, this relationship is a precious gift.

"In one sense, this relationship with my stepmother, Mary, makes me feel peaceful, because I know that my father is happy. In another way, I feel extremely lucky. I've got three incredible mothers—my mother, my stepmother, and my mother-in-law—who all have very different perspectives on life. They each give me a little bit of their own personalities to make me a better person."

By having her stepdaughter, Melanie, and Melanie's mother in her life, Karla has grown to understand "family" in a much broader sense. Karla's relationships with Melanie and her mother now bring her contentment. After all the years of not accepting Melanie as a member of her family, she said, "I've learned that a family includes the people you love and welcome into your life, whether they be love or birth relations. I consider Melanie a part of my family, and I am so glad to have both her and her mother in my life."

The wonder of opening our hearts wider is that it gives us more opportunities to love and be loved. And one of the joys of stepfamily life is how often stepmothers, stepdaughters, and the rest of the family are there, when they are most needed, for those they love.

Being There for Those We Love

*"We just talk, and I listen. I'm like
Switzerland in the family—the neutral
territory. She knows she's safe with me,
and vice versa."*

—AMY, STEPDAUGHTER, AGE 30

What better feeling is there than knowing that there are people your life who will be there for you in a pinch? For me, one of the people I can always count on is my stepmother, Linda. Evidently I am not alone. What was particularly heartwarming for me as I interviewed stepmothers and stepdaughters for this book was the number of "being there" stories that they shared. Despite the many challenges of combined family life, stepmothers and stepdaughters are there for each other—encouraging each other and being present not only at critical times but also every day.

Being there for those we care about often begins with little things—small acts of love and kindness that let us know that we are special in another person's life. "My daughter tells me that Sherry always rubs and scratches her back," Jennifer, Sherry's stepdaughter, explained.

"She does those special things. She doesn't buy every-thing we desire, but what she gives comes from her heart. Sherry's added a lot to my children's lives—an extra grandma. They love being with her."

Receiving a card or note at just the right time can let us know that someone is thinking about us. Cherie, a fifty-two-year-old stepdaughter, remembers a time when her stepmother was there for her in a very simple, yet profound, way.

"I really was struggling at the time," Cherie remem-bered. "I was living in this little one-bedroom apart-ment; my two daughters were living with their dad for the year. I was in a very bad way and I needed help. Out of the blue, I received a card of encouragement from my stepmother. It turned me around." This gesture was particularly precious to Cherie because her relationship with her stepmother had been strained for a long time; they rarely even spoke to each other.

Encouragement can come in many different ways—a smile, a wink, a thumbs-up sign. When it comes from someone we love, it is often all we need to risk doing something new, or to return to a passion that we may have left behind.

Cathleen, a twenty-nine-year-old singer in Los Angeles, credits her stepmother, Sue, with nurturing her desire to entertain. "Sue was always very creative,"

Cathleen remembers. "She would sing and act. I loved performing with her. We both love music and love going to see musicals. I just recently put a band together, and she is so proud of me. Sue is my biggest supporter."

Encouragement from a special person not only can help move us into something we love, it can also help us return to a love we've left behind. Marla's father lost his passion for music when his wife of twenty-five years went through a ten-year battle with cancer. As he journeyed with his wife through that difficult time, his friend Ruth, who eventually became Marla's stepmother, was an important source of support and encouragement.

"My father is an artist, a musician," Marla said emphatically. "His whole thing is music, but with my mom's illness, he stopped playing music for ten years. Ruth encouraged him to go back and start the band and to live that life again."

Sometimes people are there throughout our lives with just the right words of encouragement or advice at just the right time. "My stepmom, Diane, has taught me so much about life," twenty-three-year-old Ariel said. "She's always been the one who has listened to me when my dad has not been able to express himself. She was the one who reminded me that I was intelligent and beautiful. 'Stop worrying about making everyone else happy. Make yourself happy,' she would say. That's our strength: we can talk about anything and she always encourages me."

Diane loves the fact that Ariel is there for her too. Ariel says, "We both are there for each other on a equal level. I'm there when she needs someone. I love it when she comes to me and confides in me. When things get a little difficult and Diane is frustrated with my dad or just needs to vent, I like being there for her. We both understand him. It's really important to us both that we can listen to each other."

Listening to each other is also important to Amy and her stepmother, Mary. Amy, age twenty, especially enjoys being a sounding board for Mary. As she puts it, "We just talk, and I listen. I'm like Switzerland in the family—the neutral territory. She knows she's safe with me, and vice versa."

Stepmothers and stepdaughters who are there for each other in the small things are also often there for major life events—like turning sixteen. Lynda shared a bit about the "sweet sixteen" celebration she and her husband put on for Beth, her stepdaughter.

"Beth was trying to lose some weight before her sweet sixteen," Linda remembered. "I told her I would help her do it, and finally, after weeks, she reached her goal. She looked gorgeous, and I took her to shop for a beautiful new dress."

The day was important for Beth because it celebrated her becoming a woman and an adult. But more than that, she hoped she might gain the attention of one special boy.

"Her father and I threw her a big party at a nice hotel with all of her schoolmates. It was lavish and wonderful. The boy she had a crush on all year came, but didn't show any special interest in her. Her heart was broken. She thought that if she looked beautiful and was having this great party that he would like her. I was there to comfort her through such a huge teenage disappointment."

As much as they might like to, stepmoms can't protect their stepdaughters from painful times. They can, however, provide them with needed information and important advice, as well as just be with them.

"When Louise, my stepdaughter, had her babies," Renée said, "I was the one who went to the hospital with her. She counted on me for advice. It was a special time because long before we had talked about where babies come from. I have tried to always be there for her, no matter what."

Birth seems to be a common time that stepmothers are there for their stepdaughters. "When I had my daughter," Becky, a twenty-seven-year old stepdaughter, shared, "I remember how happy Teresa was to have a granddaughter. Through the births of all my children, she's been there. Whatever I wanted to eat, she would bring for me, because I always hated that hospital food. She always brings me flowers, cards, and little gifts. It's these little things that remind me how lucky I am to have her in my life. Although the circumstances weren't the best at the beginning, I think that everything happens for a reason. Right now, having Teresa to talk to always makes me feel supported and loved."

This kind of love and support can be especially important in the delivery room. "Kelly was very insecure when she went into the delivery room," Susan, a fifty-year-old stepmother, remembered. "She was sobbing because she didn't know if she would be a good mother, but I was there with her. That helped."

It is in times of crisis, perhaps, that we most appreciate having someone with us. They may not be able to remove our fear, confusion, grief, or uncertainty, but they do let us know that we are loved—and not alone. That can be a great gift, especially for children.

"I knew that I loved my stepkids," Caroline said, "but there was a pivotal moment when what that meant became crystal clear. My seven-year-old stepdaughter, Ashley, was having a slumber party. All the little girls wanted to be around me because I was young. I wasn't the typical mom. A couple of the girls came up and said, 'I wish you were my mom. You're fun.' The next thing I knew, Ashley was crying hysterically. 'It's not fair,' she said. 'They all have mothers. I don't have a mother. They don't need another mother. They can't have you too.' That was a pivotal point in my relationship with her, recognizing her neediness and realizing how I needed to be aware of it."

Listening carefully, as Caroline did for Ashley, always makes people feel like we are there for them. It is a way to show we care. Jill, age twenty-three, remembered a difficult time in her life and how important it was that her stepmother, Sue, could listen to her. "I was freaking out," she said, "questioning life and death. I started thinking I was crazy. Sue came up to me, put her arm around me, and calmed me down without saying anything. She just let me cry. It was exactly what I needed at the time. 'It's okay to be sad. Let it run its course,' she said. No one else could have brought me out of it. Going to bed that night, I felt like a dark cloud had been lifted.

"I think the reason I was so comfortable going to her," Jill continued, "is that she is a psychologist. She's a wonderful sounding board. She welcomes ideas and thoughts about how I am feeling and what's going on.

She understands things very quickly. She says it's like a therapy session, but it's not gooey. She's like a friend-mom-psychiatrist all in one."

All types of experiences can precipitate a crisis. A common one is the pressure of school. Faith, age twenty-three, recalls, "Lesley was a major support system for me when I was in school, especially when I was flipping out about writing papers or taking tests. She sat with me at the computer many a night and helped me type the papers."

When love relationships reach a critical point, there's no one better to turn to than someone who loves and cares for us. Someone to be there when we feel alone can make all the difference. "I was going through a really bad thing with my boyfriend," Faith remembered, "and I was really depressed. Lesley sat me down in front of the fire; we got some wine, cheese, and crackers; and I just cried and cried. She let me be me. I got it all out and was fine after that."

Sometimes simply being there during a crisis can offer people the strength to believe that they will get through it. "My stepdaughter, Jill, told me that when she went through her hard times in college and lost her way for a while, I was one of the people who really helped her through it," Sue remembers. "She said that I was not only there for her, but I also gave her the confidence to know that everything would be okay. Having previously been a psychologist in the college system, I knew that the identity crisis she was going through was not uncommon, so I could confidently tell her that she would be alright."

Unfortunately, crises do not always affect only one person in a relationship at a time. When both stepmother and stepdaughter are going through difficult times, they may struggle to find ways to mutually support one another. "My stepdaughter, Katie, had a long-distance boyfriend in high school," Jeannette, fifty-two, remembered. "During the summer, they went to the same camp for two months. When she came home, she missed him terribly. I was really patient with her the first few days back, and was being as supportive as I could be, though she was being difficult, which is unlike her. I ended up losing my patience with her one day in the kitchen. I slammed my hand on the table and said, 'Katie, I need you to do better than this. My father may be dying.' I needed her to take a look at the bigger picture and I told her so. She looked at me and said, 'I'll do better. I promise.' And she did. By being honest with our feelings, we were able to be there for each other."

Sometimes the first time a person is there for us is a memorable one, as it was for Kerry. Kerry, age thirty-six, had had almost no contact with her father for years, and she had only recently met Donna, her stepmother. One day Kerry and Donna were looking through Donna's family photo albums.

"My dad was real big on archiving family photos," Kerry remembered. "As I looked through page after page, I realized that there was not one picture of the two of us—not even one picture of me—in this whole album. I felt like I didn't exist. Donna could tell something was wrong. 'Are you alright?' she asked. I blurted out, 'No! I'm not okay. I'm not even in this album, not one page, not even any mention of me. It's like I'm not a part of this family. There are people in here that Dad's never even met. How can this be?' She held me and said, 'It's not that, it's not that. There are other albums that are *just* of you.'" Kerry paused and added, "In that moment, she was there for me. It still really affects me, because we didn't have too many moments together before this one."

The feeling of being left out is a painful one. To have someone reassure us that we won't be or haven't been abandoned is a great gift. Caroline made an effort to show her stepdaughter and stepson that, although their biological mother had left them, she never would abandon them. One of the ways she did this was by taking concrete actions for them.

"My stepchildren's mother left them, and she had a lot of other problems," Caroline said. "I knew they were afraid that one day I might leave too, so I started planning the birthday parties. I started buying the birthday and Christmas presents. I started making sure that they had certain things for school. They could rely on me. When I said I'd do something, I'd do it. They could see that I'd be there for them."

Difficult situations, such as unexpected pregnancies, often bring out the best in stepmothers. Sometimes it is just this kind of situation that helps stepdaughters appreciate their stepmothers in a new and deeper way.

Sherry's stepdaughter, Jennifer, remembers the time Sherry was really there for her. "Our difficult relationship didn't really change until I was sixteen and became pregnant with my daughter. My mother kicked me out. Sherry was the only one who stepped forward to give my daughter a baby shower. I know that was the turning point in our relationship. Although she didn't think my getting pregnant was the right decision nor did she want to condone it, she felt I was still her stepdaughter. She actually treated me like I was her daughter. She said she wanted to support me any way she could. She was there for me in such a special way—when no one else was. I will never forget how she was there for me."

Cynthia, age forty-five, also supported her step-daughter, Janeen, when she unexpectedly became pregnant and prepared to marry. Even though their relationship was somewhat strained, that did not interfere with Cynthia's ability to step in and handle the coordination of Janeen's wedding day. "Janeen was pregnant and was upset already. She wasn't going to have the dream wedding that she had always hoped for. She still didn't know what she was going to wear. I was having the wedding at my house and was even making the cake. I had my hands literally full. But when Janeen suggested we go to the mall, I willingly went and helped her pick out a dress. I realized later that Janeen felt like she needed me."

Janeen has her own memories of that time. "Cynthia was the one who suggested having the wedding at her house, and when I needed a wedding dress and shoes, it was Cynthia who took me," she said. "I was feeling so fat and gross and sad because I knew I wasn't going to be wearing a pretty, lacy white dress, like the one I always wanted to be married in. We went to the maternity store and Cynthia picked out the dress. It was feminine and pretty, and then we had a great time shopping for shoes. It was a terrific bonding experience for the both of us. The night before the wedding, I slept at Cynthia and Dad's house. Cynthia used to work in a bakery, so she applied her baking talents to the creation of a beautiful three-layer cake. During the ceremony, my father played guitar and Cynthia sang "The Wedding Song." She did so much to make the wedding as beautiful as possible. I will never forget how special she made it for my husband and me."

Being there for each other during a time of serious illness is another sign of a strong stepfamily. Marla's mother had been ill for ten years, and toward the end of her life was in a convalescent hospital. Marla recalls, "Ruth, my future stepmother, came into my dad's life during my mother's illness. She is a beautiful, vivacious woman—the kind of person my father needed to be with at this time."

Marla's father had been a caregiver to his ailing wife for so many years and had given so much of himself for so long that Ruth's presence was an enormous grace. "We've always been so thankful for her. She came into our lives at a difficult time and made an incredible difference," Marla says. The last few months of Marla's mom's life, Ruth was the anchor. Marla remembers, "Ruth and my dad were at the hospital every single day—with Ruth waiting in the lobby while my dad went to see my mom. She would say to us, 'This is where you need to be. This is what you need to do.' Ruth stepped into their lives at a pivotal time and shed light on a dark and painful experience. Deeply affected by Ruth's unselfishness and encouragement, Marla confides, "She's just an amazing lady. I look up to her."

In one very unusual situation, a stepdaughter was helped by a stepmother she hadn't even known she had. Though she had little other contact with him, Erin's father usually was in touch with her for her birthday and Christmas. One year, when she was in college, he didn't send a birthday message. When he finally called, a week or more later, he still wanted to get together. Erin put him off, but, as she puts it, "He started being very insistent about getting together. We met for lunch, during which he said, 'I really need to tell you this,' and he pulled out a picture of the cutest little six-year-old boy. 'This is your half brother,' he said. I was completely in shock!" Although Erin had had absolutely no indication of his remarriage, her father and stepmother had actually been married for eighteen years.

Erin eventually did meet her stepmother, Shirley. Unfortunately, that was shortly before her father died. She was left with many questions without answers. Erin cried as she told her story. Then she took a deep breath and said, "I have come to accept what happened, even though I have many questions that only my father could have answered. I'm going on with my life. Shirley and I were virtual strangers. Now she is in my life. She is family. I really don't know how I would have gotten through the passing of my father without her. I think we were sent to help each other during this period."

The wonder of stepmothers is that sometimes they can be there for their stepdaughters in ways that their fathers cannot. Stepping in as a confidante and a friend, stepmothers can often be more objective and accepting than biological parents. Because of this, stepmothers sometimes become the first one their stepdaughters seek out to express sadness, fear, or even happiness. This was the case for Zanetha, when she shared some wonderful, but potentially disconcerting, news with her stepmother, Joi.

"When I told Joi I was head-over-heels in love, she was thrilled for me. When I told her that I had met my girlfriend just a couple of weeks earlier, but I knew this was it, Joi was radiant. She had such joy on her face, but she had to control it because my father walked in just as I went to embrace her."

Joi's unrestrained happiness for Zanetha gave Zanetha the courage to share her news with her father. Zanetha continued, "Unable to control myself, I just let my guts spill right there—with my father too. When I had seen Joi's reaction—she was literally jumping up and down—I really felt like my dad would support me. I looked at Dad and told him I was in love with a woman. He paused. A look of panic crossed his face. I quickly turned to Joi and she was beaming. Dad didn't know what to do, but then he realized my happiness. He couldn't deny me that. He smiled and reached his hands out to me, 'Okay,' he said."

When Joi accepted her completely without any kind of hesitation, Zanetha knew that her relationship with Joi had just jumped to the next level. Zanetha explained, "She totally understands the female psyche and the female connection. She was able to give me an unconditional out pouring of love that even my dad and I didn't share. Joi and I have had a deep connection ever since."

These wonderful, heart-warming stories reflect the wonder of being there for those we love. I was delighted when, during the interview process itself, women began to realize how often their stepmothers and stepdaughters supported them. Reflecting on their lives together, many of these women felt inspired to call and remind their steps how much they have meant to them. Without a doubt, being there when someone needs us is a gift that lasts a lifetime—for those we love and for us as well.

Delight

Gathering the Gifts
of Life Together

The intimacy of the stepmother-stepdaughter relationship is reflected in the wealth of life experiences they share. Sometimes these experiences are difficult and painful; often they are challenging and growth-filled. When stepmothers and stepdaughters reflect on their shared lives, however, they also acknowledge the gifts they have received—and there is deep delight in this.

"Delight" not only means joy or something that gives great pleasure, it also means the feeling of a high degree of gratification. Delight, then, emerges not only from easy and good times together, it also comes from times of challenge, change, and growth. Often only in retrospect can the true gifts of those times be recognized and acknowledged.

In this section, stepmothers and stepdaughters share stories of letting go—of guilt, anger, hurt, difficulty, and personal desires—and choosing love. They also reflect on the mysteries of life—of giving, receiving, questions unanswered, lives touched—that have added an unexpectedly rich dimension to their time together. And finally, they share stories that celebrate their love for each other and the delight that they have gathered in their relationships as stepmothers and stepdaughters.

Letting Go and Choosing Love

"I realized that love isn't flawless.
Now I could see my father and stepmother
as they really are—and love them anyway."

—ERIN, STEPDAUGHTER, AGE 34

Letting go may be one of the hardest emotional tasks that stepmothers and stepdaughters face. Holding on— to anger, resentment, others' expectations, and more—is a very human attribute. But in many cases holding on often means shutting out, a lesson stepmothers and stepdaughters have learned well. Very consciously, though not always easily, they choose to let go as a means of inclusion, not exclusion. By choosing to let go, they give themselves the opportunity to love.

Zanetha benefited from another person's letting go— her father's. "My father lives in a little river town in Ohio, where he was viewed as the 'man about town,'" Zanetha said. But that all changed when he met Zanetha's future stepmother, Joi. "She is so sweet and dear and loving and kind," Zanetha explained. "She is the woman who encouraged him to grow. She is a major nurturer; she gives and gives and gives. I feel that he is lucky to have her." Zanetha, too, feels lucky to have Joi in her life—all because her father was able to let go of his old ways and choose love.

Letting go may also mean putting our priorities in order. For most of us, clarifying our lives is a major challenge. Stacey, however, made a concerted effort to spend a special time with her stepmother, Mary, even in the midst of a crazed week. For Mary, having this time with Stacey was a wonderful and unexpected gift.

Mary and her husband, Stacey's father, had flown to Vermont to visit Stacey and her new husband, Darren, who had just returned from their honeymoon. "I'll never forget the day we arrived," Mary remembers. "Stacey was having fifty people over to celebrate her upcoming graduation from medical school, getting ready to move into her medical residency, and packing for their move to another state. She had all of this going on, and she still took a day to surprise me with a trip to Maine. I remember I said, 'You don't have time,' and Stacey said, 'Yes, I do! I'm doing it!' That's what made me feel so good—the fact she took the time to be with me."

Stacey remembers the thrill of having time alone with Mary: "We went antiquing, and since we were in Maine, I couldn't let her get away without having a Maine lobster on the coast. I thought she would really love that. We talked the whole time, which was wonderful because we never get to talk like that—no interruptions for the entire day. It was fun. She has always been there for me, so it was nice that I could reciprocate. I would do it again in a heartbeat."

In another kind of letting go, Diane and Ariel chose an unknown path—all because of Ariel's love of a sport and the possibility of personal growth.

Diane remembered, "Ariel was in high school. She started playing soccer at an older age than usual, but she was so good that she was quickly promoted to varsity. However, she was probably going to be sitting on the bench an awful lot. She agonized over whether she should go with the varsity soccer team, a much higher level, or stay one of the stars of junior varsity. We encouraged her to go for the varsity spot. We felt it could teach her about reaching a bit over her head with the confidence that she could possibly do it. That year she received the award for the most improved player! She really grew from the experience."

Another stepdaughter, Cherie, learned to let go of her feelings of guilt for not being there when her stepmother needed her. "She was having a hysterectomy," Cherie remembers, "and I wasn't there to support her. We were so angry with her at the time that my sister and I didn't even show up at the hospital. I was nineteen and I really didn't understand what she was going through."

Cherie paused, then continued. "Now that I am a parent, I understand what a self-sacrifice it is to be a mother, especially when the children are not your biological kids. You give up a lot—and you gain a lot. It takes so much time and energy. Forgiveness is essential. Just being able to get to that place of acceptance, unconditional love, and forgiveness on all parts, that is the healer." In letting go of her feelings of guilt, Cherie moved toward a new level of self-acceptance and self-love.

Unfortunately, letting go usually isn't a simple, one-time affair. It can take continual effort over a long period of time, especially when it involves a relationship with a history of difficulty, as it did for Teresa and Becky. "My stepdaughter, Becky, and I have had a very difficult time," Teresa said. "I think that she loves and respects me, but it hasn't been easy. Despite the challenges, I realize how important my relationship is with her. I need to spend time with her, and to let her know how much she and our relationship mean to me. We've both been trying really hard to do that more—and to let go of the past."

Like Teresa and Becky, Erin also reaped the benefits of letting go of anger and hurt. With only occasional contact with her father (usually on her birthday and Christmas), Erin felt betrayed and bereft of a family she never knew existed, when her father revealed he had remarried eighteen years earlier. By the time she met her stepmother, Shirley, Erin's father was close to death.

Erin had many unanswered questions that now, because of her father's illness and impending death, would never be answered: Why didn't he tell her about his marriage and child? Why, for so long, had she been cheated out of being part of this family? Why did Shirley choose to stay in a relationship with her father, even though his alcoholism contributed to his fatal illness? Finally, Erin said, "I took a step back and decided that no matter what he said, I would never really know why he didn't tell me. I realized that love isn't flawless. Now I could see my father and stepmother as they really are—and love them anyway."

Being able to love is often the fruit of letting go. Making that decision is not always easy, but it is freeing. We may not even realize how we were able to do it, but somehow—perhaps out of hope for a better relationship or because of some previously untapped inner strength—we manage to let go and choose love. In doing so, we are touched by a mystery of life, one of the unexpected yet simply gracious gifts of relationship. In the next chapter, stepmothers and stepdaughters will share a bit more about their experiences with the mysteries of life and how they learned to welcome them.

Embracing Mysteries of Life

"If you really care for and love a child, . . .
you will see that relationship unfold into
a beautiful thing. You must . . . trust in it."

— SUE, STEPMOTHER, AGE 50

When we think of mysteries, several things may come to mind: a whodunit novel, how a sock disappears in the laundry, or, perhaps, a spiritual truth that cannot be fully understood. The mysteries of everyday life—especially in the special relationships between stepmothers and stepdaughters—may include elements of each of these. Like the whodunit, we know something is going on, but we're not sure what—and we won't know till end of the story. Like the missing sock, we're dealing with something very basic and ordinary—frustrating when it's not in place but often taken for granted when it is. And like a spiritual truth, we experience moments in our lives that, while quite ordinary, push the edges of our hearts, our minds, and our very understanding of life, ourselves, and each other.

These experiences of mystery—some of which we approach with reluctance and others that we embrace with open arms—can be quite simple or quite profound. They touch us deeply and leave us grateful for the experience.

One of the wonderful mysteries in Monica's life is her stepmother's intuition, her ability to know just when to be in touch or when to send a special little gift. "Leah," Monica says, "is a highly intuitive person. She'll know when I am having a bad day, even though we haven't spoken and she is on the other side of the country." This stepmother and stepdaughter understand that small efforts have big impact. Monica added, "She'll send a card for Easter along with an Easter basket filled with jacks and Chinese checkers, cute little fun things to play with—just because."

The mystery of seemingly little actions is that they can have a lasting effect. In Jennifer's case, it is precisely her stepmother's actions that have impressed Jennifer over the years. Jennifer said, "The biggest effect Sherry's had in my life is to *show* me and not *tell* me—to show me that you can turn a bad situation into a good one through patience and perseverance and by believing in yourself. She's affected my life by giving me a lot of those qualities. What I admire about her is that she never presses it on me. She's very supportive and demonstrates these things instead of using words and talking, talking, talking."

But sometimes words combined with actions—and a good dose of humor—can lovingly move someone toward a deeper self-acceptance that can benefit the entire family. Deena always had fond feelings for her stepmother, Patti. However, it wasn't until she saw the unique way in which Patti handled a very sensitive issue with her father that she came to realize just how special Patti was to her father and the family.

"Patti," thirty-year-old Deena said, "was determined to get rid of Dad's toupee. He's worn a toupee all his life and refused to take it off in public. Patti worked on him, reminding him in her sweet and gentle way to just be himself. So Christmas came around and we were lounging about in our pajamas. Dad had put his toupee on the bathroom counter, and when Patti went in to brush her teeth, she decided to have a little fun. She came out of the bathroom with the toupee stuck on her crotch. 'Look,' Patti exclaimed, 'you can use it for this,' she placed it under her arm and said, 'or this,' and she continued dancing around the room with the thing. We were all laughing hysterically. It was the funniest thing I had ever seen. I looked at Dad and he was laughing too. I realized I totally loved this woman. She was so real. She was able to get my dad to laugh at himself, which is something I had never seen before."

Just as laughter can carry us into the realm of mystery,

so can tears. Erin, whose father had kept his marriage to her stepmother secret for eighteen years, was left with many unanswered questions after his death. "I was never close to Shirley, and I didn't understand the nature of their relationship. I thought I'd never met her before my father's confession, but Shirley told me we had met when I was only two years old. She was very sensitive to my feelings and approached the situation with such sweetness—she hugged me, held me, and let me cry. Then I asked her, 'Why? Why didn't I get a chance to know you sooner?' After a very long pause, she said, 'You know what? I don't know.' I knew then that Shirley and I had just experienced a life-changing moment. I will never forget it. We looked at each other and really saw each other for the first time."

Throughout their lives, stepmothers and stepdaughters have these moments of seeing "for the first time." Sometimes such epiphanies come with the realization that we have positively influenced, perhaps unexpectedly, the life of another.

One aspect of Mary's influence on her stepdaughter, Amy, was shown in a simple, yet heartwarming, way. "Amy is now engaged and living in San Francisco. Her father, Jim, and I went up there for the first time to see her home. When we got there, Amy and her fiancé offered us hors d'oeuvres and a bottle of champagne. It was so nice. Like my other stepdaughter, Stacey, Amy copies things I do. Her bedroom is set up in the same way as mine. Just like me, she has little things around the house. When I'm in her home, I'm always saying, 'This is just like me!' It makes me feel wonderful."

Other times the proof of the stepmother's effect on her stepdaughter's life is more subtle, such as the gratification that comes from seeing her grow into a healthy, productive adult. "When you start to see the 'payoff,'" as Diane put it, "you aren't looking to get something back. Instead, the payoff is seeing that your children are okay and that you've helped them to thrive as individuals. Both my stepdaughters are exceptional women—women you'd want to know. To know that I'm a part of it, and then have them actually appreciate me, is like icing on the cake."

A particularly wonderful mystery is the transformation of a life. Gloria, whose stepdaughter, Stephanie, had significant emotional and substance abuse problems when they met, is rightfully proud of the influence she's had on Stephanie's life.

"I have seen so many relationships that don't begin to match the quality of the relationship I have with Stephanie," Gloria said. "I have a great deal of pride about it because she has turned out to be such a lovely young woman, wife, and mother. The truth is I am *very* proud. It's hard for me to pat myself on the back—ask anyone who knows me—but I know I made a difference in her life."

Knowing that one has significantly improved the life of a child can be very satisfying. More than that, it may give a stepmother a sense of her place in the world and reassure her that she is doing something very worthwhile. "I feel my role as mother and stepmother is so important," Kathy says. "It's not just because I decided to have children, but because of the positive influence I can have on my stepkids. It's amazing how you can change people's lives—and how they can change yours."

Lynda believes that her role as a stepmother can best be described like this: "It makes me feel like God put me on Earth for something. That is why I feel I am here—to be in Beth's life. I was here to give her what she has needed to become a whole person. She has definitely given me much to look at too. I've been changed because of it. You always feel better when you are giving than when you are taking, but having Beth in my life has given me so much. I feel appreciated."

Perhaps one of the greatest mysteries of all is how we can have a positive influence on someone's life without our even knowing it, as in the relationship of Melanie and her stepmother, Karla. Though for many years Karla didn't really want to find a place for Melanie in her "picture-perfect" family, she never made Melanie feel unwanted or unloved. Karla rose above her own reluctance and created a place for Melanie.

"I have seen so many families clearly divided," Melanie commented. "Those kinds of relationships are made up of people who just exist with one another and who tolerate each other because of circumstance. I feel lucky that my situation isn't like that. I feel so fortunate to have Karla in my life."

Love, even a love she didn't know she had, allowed Karla to create a place for Melanie in her life. Now they share a connection that they hadn't realized was possible. Sue summed up this mysterious love between a stepmother and stepdaughter in these words: "This relationship makes me feel gratified. It makes me feel right—like this was the right thing to do, that it was worth all the time invested. All of the patience was worth it. I think if you really care for and love a child, even when they're teenagers and not as easy, you will see that relationship unfold into a beautiful thing. You must believe that you can trust in it." This, perhaps, is the greatest mystery of all—love.

Celebrating Our Love

*"I . . . realize how much I appreciate
my stepmother. I'm going to go home,
write her a note, and tell her."*

—LISA, STEPDAUGHTER, AGE 29

One of the great delights in the lives of stepmothers and stepdaughters is the love they share for each other. Some stepmothers and stepdaughters may have literally grown up together, while others have come together as adults. The shape of these stepmother-stepdaughter relationships may vary, but their intimate connection—sometimes easily woven, sometimes hard-won—gathers together the many shared experiences of their lives. In the stories that follow, we celebrate those experiences and the love that strengthens them all.

When stepmothers and stepdaughters reflect on the love they share, it is often particular acts of caring—sometimes small, sometime large—that they talk about. These concrete acts are signs of the deeper, ongoing love that binds them in relationship with each other.

Stacey talks about how her stepmother, Mary, loves to pamper her family members.

"She's always doing things for the family—like my thirtieth surprise birthday party. I was given a massage—I knew that particular gift was a 'Mary' idea—but while I was in the other room, all these people showed up. Mary brought my mom down and my grandmother, as well as my dad's mom and sister, and my sister, Amy. It was a huge surprise. When I came out, I saw all of my friends and family standing there. I said thank you to my dad and he said, 'It was Mary.' I gave each of them a big hug."

Sometimes stepmothers give gifts that stepdaughters don't receive from anyone else, which makes them feel especially appreciated. "For Valentine's Day," Jennifer shared, "Sherry was the only person who gave me flowers. My kids gave me things, but she was the only adult who brought me flowers—in three colors, no less. That made me so happy. In return, she was so pleased that I was happy to receive them! She realized how much the flowers meant to me, so the appreciation went both ways." Jennifer paused, then added, "Sherry was sensitive to me and to my needs. The choices I have made haven't been easy, but she's stood by my side and has made these wonderful gestures—to show me support."

One of the attributes of love is its generosity—it allows people to love even more. Faith experienced this kind of love from her stepmother, Lesley, when Lesley nurtured Faith's relationship with her boyfriend in a concrete way. This particular act of love came during a family trip to Florida. Faith, along with her boyfriend, Rob, had joined Lesley and Faith's father, her grandparents, and her stepbrother for a vacation.

"My family would spend the day together at the beach and the pool," Faith remembered. "Then we would all go onto the balcony and watch the sun set. Everything we did was family oriented. Grandpa was sort of getting possessive of me, wanting to teach me the family trade, and encouraging me to take over as director one day. In the meantime, Rob and I hadn't had any time alone.

"I had just gotten up one morning when Lesley told me that she was going to take Grandpa away for the day, so Rob and I could go off and do whatever we wanted to do. She said, 'Pack up a breakfast, pack up a lunch. Take a walk on the beach. You guys have the whole day to yourself. I know you've been patiently waiting, and I know how he loves you. It's time you guys spend some time alone.' Of course we really wanted it, but I hadn't said anything, nor had Rob. It was this wonderful little miracle she gave us and it meant a lot to me."

Loving actions, such as Lesley's, have a certain contagious quality to them: one often leads to others.

Marla remembers how special her stepmother, Ruth, can make a dinner. "She'll invite us for simple family dinners, and she will set the table beautifully," Marla says, smiling. "We'll sit in the dining room with flowers and candles. As I look at the table, I think to myself, 'What a nice idea. I'm going to do that. In fact, I'm going to do that every night.'"

By bringing beauty into the lives of those she loves, Ruth expresses her tenderness and affection for them. Her beautifully set table is a celebration of her love and appreciation for Marla and the rest of her family.

Sometimes, however, we think we may have to wait a while to receive that appreciation. We can, however, be pleasantly surprised, as Sue was. "I always thought that I was a really good stepmother," Sue said, "but I thought I would have to wait until Jill was forty years old for her to realize it. That's not because of who she is as a person, but because that's how long it normally takes for most people. Yet she's so appreciative of me now. She recognizes things at twenty-three that I thought it would take much longer for her to see. Not only is the appreciation wonderful, but being able to see the growth in our relationship is extremely rewarding for me."

Friendship is one of the benefits of the stepmother-stepdaughter relationship for Patti, and yet their relationship goes beyond that. "I know we are more than friends. I didn't have to parent them, so it's entirely different than other people's experience. We have honesty and humor—they even get my humor!" Patti said, laughing. Then more seriously, she added, "I respect them and they respect me. They are very verbal about their feelings for me. They tell me how much they love me all the time."

Love is celebrated through the sharing of friendship, honesty, humor, respect, and feelings. It is also celebrated by the desire to do something good for each other. Because of all the wonderful things that her stepmother, Joi, has done for her, Zanetha has a strong desire to give back.

"If I could do something for her right now," Zanetha says, "I would love to spend time with her one-on-one, alone. If I had the money, I'd take her to a spa and just pamper her for a week. She wouldn't have to deal with her kids or her husband. I would take care of everything. I would pay for all her bills while she wasn't working and make sure she got massaged every day. She gives every day, all day, to someone; she's always there giving all of her energy. I would love to see her get some of that back."

Even when it's not possible, financially or otherwise, to do the wonderful things we'd like to do for someone we love, the desire to do so reveals a deep love and appreciation. But sometimes expressing that love and appreciation can be as simple as writing a note, as it was for Lisa.

As I was interviewing Lisa, I had no idea that her talking about her life with her stepmother, Diane, was profoundly affecting her. Suddenly it seemed as if a rush of feelings came over her. Then she said something that touched me very deeply. "I think you just made me realize how much I appreciate my stepmother," Lisa said quietly. "I'm going to go home, write her a note, and tell her."

The love of stepmothers and stepdaughters extends beyond the relationship that originally brought them together. Mary explained, "I know if anything ever happened to their dad, my stepdaughters and I would still be in touch. They say all the time how much they love me, how I am so good to them. I know it is a mutual bond, a mutual love that we have, and that gives us all strength."

Love is a bond that gives strength—and much more. "My relationship with my stepmother," Katie says, "makes me feel lucky and appreciated. I feel like it has made me a stronger person. Knowing that I can maintain healthy relationships with four parents and keep everyone close to me in ways that I could never have imagined possible, makes me feel that I'm okay all of the time."

Katie's sentiments sum up what many of the women I interviewed tried to express. Their love, as these stories have shown over and over again, is vibrant and real. In a world where often there is too little love, that shared by stepmothers, stepdaughters, and their whole families is certainly a love to celebrate.

Conclusion

In the lives of stepmothers, stepdaughters, and step-families, the conclusion to a book such as this is not the end. Instead, we come to another beginning. I hope that the stories shared here will inspire you to a new beginning of freshness, new perspectives, and hope, as well as a sense that you are not alone in this challenging and fulfilling experience of combined family living. Above all, I hope you feel acknowledged and affirmed for your generous commitment and hard work in creating a family.

As I mentioned earlier in the book, we need to remember that love brings families together. A woman and a man fall in love, then choose to share their lives and join their families. Though brokenness of one type or another (usually divorce or death) can precede their marriage, it is love that sustains and nourishes family members as this new family is birthed. It is love—in its fullest and most resilient sense—that enables us to discover and learn as we live together each day, to deepen our courage as we face new challenges, to dare to create new ways of being family, and to delight in the gifts of life together. At its best, that love is like a pebble dropping in a pond, rippling outward in ever-widening circles, touching and embracing more and more lives.

That love touches our lives in concrete ways each days we live together. What we need to openly acknowledge—first for ourselves and then in the wider community—is that stepfamilies can be, and often are, healthy and happy families. As we've seen in many of the stories shared here, stepfamilies can provide a stable, secure, and loving environment for children and adults alike. As Karla, a stepmother, put it, "Families are what you make them," and the reality is that many stepparents and stepchildren work very hard to create a loving, nurturing home. We need to recognize, acknowledge, and, perhaps most important of all, *celebrate* this hard yet creative work that stepmothers, stepdaughters, and all members of stepfamilies do each day. Although we can't deny that stepfamilies may have problems, and serious ones at that—in this they are no different than many nuclear families—we need to affirm the good that has often been neglected. We want to affirm the kind of step relationship that inspires Lisa to say about her stepmother, Diane, "The amount of effort she put into making me happy was enormous. She has been a huge influence in my life."

We know—from our own experience and from the life stories shared here—that many challenges face stepfamilies. But we also know that the combining of families offers wonderful opportunities for the development of personal and family flexibility, attitudes of generosity and cooperation, and openness to new perspectives and new ways of doing things. These are healthy-family qualities that transcend the boundaries of nuclear and nonnuclear families. They are, at heart, qualities of balanced and humane human beings, which, hopefully, every family seeks to nurture.

Creating loving, stable homes in which children and adults alike can thrive and grow is not a luxury; it is a necessity. A loving, supportive environment significantly raises the odds that children will grow into healthy, contributing members of society—and if they have children, their experience in a loving, caring environment will set the tone for yet another generation.

Family work is important work, and the relationships of stepmothers and stepdaughters, as well as entire step-families, are an integral part of that work. Too often we forget that the health of the family is built upon the things we do, or try to do, every day: loving, caring for, and respecting each other; resolving conflicts and solving problems; building relationships in physically and emotionally safe home environments; keeping hope alive and encouraging each other to reach new heights; supporting those we love through good times and bad. All of this, of course, comes on top of cooking, cleaning, doing laundry, getting groceries, chauffeuring the kids, and all the other necessities of family life! Together—moment by moment, day by day—stepmothers, stepdaughters, and stepfamilies are doing these things, and more. Together we—*you*—strive to create happy and healthy families that are a gift to our families themselves and for our larger society as well. Thank you for all you have done and continue to do!

I hope, if even in little ways, this book has helped you feel supported, affirmed, and befriended in your lives as stepmothers and stepdaughters. I hope you will find ways to celebrate the love and life you share. Though you were brought into your own stepmother-stepdaughter relationship by chance, may you be deep and loving friends for a lifetime.

Sharing Our Wisdom

Advice to Steps and Soon-to-Be Steps

Stepmothers Speak to Stepmothers

"You must accept these children as the number-one priority in your life. *Everything* else is secondary."
—CAROLINE

❁

"Don't attempt to mother them. Just be yourself."
—SUSAN

❁

"Sit down together, and think and talk about what a step relationship is going to mean." —KARLA

❁

"Know when to go for a walk instead of getting upset. Talk with friends who have been through stepparenting themselves." —DIANE

❁

"Try to do everything in the children's best interests, as opposed to your own selfish interests." —KATHY

❁

"Be as positive an influence as you can possibly be."
—GLORIA

"You have to let go." —Renée

✿

"Get your agenda out of the way. Whatever you think of this child, whatever you think of the mother, get over it. Just drop it. If there is an issue, drop it." —Judith

✿

"Have someone to talk to about where you are with yourself and your own feelings about being a step-mother. Think about what your role truly is." —Sue

✿

"Make your own way and be your own person." —Susan

✿

"Have patience. Let your relationship with your stepchildren develop naturally." —Jeannette

✿

"Be a role model." —Gloria

✿

"As with any other relationship, you've got to make an investment." —Lesley

"You cannot control on any level whatsoever." —JUDITH

✦

"Caring for children is so important. If you need some support with it, even professional support, you should get it. It's an important job to raise children and one you should be conscious about." —CAROL

✦

"Let them come to you." —SUSAN

✦

"You have to give love to get love." —GLORIA

✦

"Learn how to take really good care of yourself." —DIANE

Stepdaughters Speak to Stepdaughters

"Just remember that your parents are human, too, and they have needs. They need to find a partner in life too." —AMY

❀

"It's scary and hard to be vulnerable, but you're both vulnerable. Be gentle with each other. It is a fragile relationship that has to be handled with care." —ARIEL

❀

"Nurture the relationship and hang in there. Give it time." —STACEY

❀

"Be friendly, fair, and honest. Try to understand where the other person is coming from." —AMY

❀

"Your stepmother is a part of your family. If you can see her as a family member, it's even more special and incredible." —DEENA

❀

"Be completely open and have no expectations." —ZANETHA

"Give it time and don't shut your stepmother out. Let her step in bit by bit, as you feel comfortable." —JILL

❖

"You may have a hard time accepting it, but this woman is going to be a benefit to your life." —JENNIFER

❖

"Communicate with your new stepmom about feelings—even negative ones. That way she might be able to better understand that your feelings are just feelings, no matter how terrible your behavior or the things you say." —MELANIE

❖

"The step relationship is a very unique and different relationship that we are not born understanding. We learn as we go, but we have to want to open ourselves up to succeeding. When we put ourselves on the line, we can get through anything." —FAITH

❖

"Keep an open mind." —LOUISE

Notes

1 Kay Pasley et al., "Successful Stepfamily Therapy: Clients' Perspectives," *Journal of Marital and Family Therapy* 22, no. 3 (July 1996) 343.

2 Mary Bloch Jones and Jo Ann Schiller, *Stepmothers: Keeping It Together with Your Husband and His Kids* (New York: Birch Lane Press, 1992) 2.

3 Ibid.

4 Kay Pasley et al., "Successful Stepfamily Therapy," 343.

5 Jane Nelson, Cheryl Erwin, and H. Stephen Glenn, *Positive Discipline for Blended Families: Nurturing Harmony, Respect, and Unity in Your New Stepfamily* (Rocklin, CA: Prima Publishing, 1997) xi.

6 Jones and Schiller, *Stepmothers: Keeping It Together with Your Husband and His Kids*, 2.

7 Nelson, Erwin, and Glenn, *Positive Discipline for Blended Families*, x.

8 Harold H. Bloomfield, M.D., with Robert Kory, *Making Peace in Your Stepfamily: Surviving and Thriving as Parents and Stepparents* (New York: Hyperion, 1993) 235.

9 Jones and Schiller, *Stepmothers Keeping It Together with Your Husband and His Kids*, 36–37.

About the Author

Karen Annarino, a Los Angeles native, began her creative career acting in live theater and television commercials. Graduating with honors from Stephen's College (Theater Arts) in Columbia, Missouri, she was involved in directing, performing, and stage managing over thirty main stage productions. She has studied under acting mentors Sandford Meisner and Jeff Goldblum at the Neighborhood Playhouse. Ms. Annarino was hired as the first American employee for the French Canadian circus, *Cirque Du Soleil*, working as a Pre-Production Director, Production Consultant, and as Assistant General Manager. Karen also worked on such productions as "The Lost City of Atlantis, a Universal theme park ride, and Siegfried and Roy's, 3D Imax Film, for Metrolight Studios. Ms. Annarino recently produced graphics for an installation at Madison Square Garden for the NHL, NBA and the WNBA. She received a Telly Award for her work.

In this book, her first, Karen blends her professional love of storytelling with a subject that is very close to her heart.

About the Press

Wildcat Canyon Press publishes books that embrace such subjects as friendship, spirituality, women's issues, and home and family, all with a focus on self-help and personal growth. Great care is taken to create books that inspire reflection and improve the quality of our lives. Our books invite sharing and are frequently given as gifts.

For a catalog of our publications, please write:
Wildcat Canyon Press
2716 Ninth Street
Berkeley, California 94710
Phone: (510) 848-3600
Fax: (510) 848-1326

Visit our website at www.wildcatcanyon.com

More Wildcat Canyon Titles . . .

LIFE AFTER BABY: FROM PROFESSIONAL WOMAN TO
BEGINNER PARENT
An emotional compass for career women navigating the
unfamiliar seas of parenthood.
Wynn McClenahan Burkett
$14.95 ISBN 1-885171-44-7

BOUNTIFUL WOMEN: LARGE WOMEN'S SECRETS FOR
LIVING THE LIFE THEY DESIRE
The definitive book for women who believe that "bounti-
ful" is a way of being in this world, not a particular size.
Bonnie Bernell
$14.95 ISBN 1-885171-47-1

AND WHAT DO YOU DO? WHEN WOMEN CHOOSE TO
STAY HOME
At last, a book for the 7.72 million women who don't
work outside the home—by choice!
Loretta Kaufman and Mary Quigley
$14.95 ISBN 1-885171-40-4

40 OVER 40: 40 THINGS EVERY WOMAN OVER 40
NEEDS TO KNOW ABOUT GETTING DRESSED
An image consultant shows women over forty how to
love what they wear and wear what they love.
Brenda Kinsel
$16.95 ISBN 1-885171-42-0

GUESS WHO'S COMING TO DINNER: CELEBRATING
CROSS-CULTURAL, INTERFAITH, AND INTERRACIAL
RELATIONSHIPS
True-life tales of the deep bonds that diversity makes.
Brenda Lane Richardson
$13.95 ISBN 1-885171-41-2

OUT OF THE BLUE: ONE WOMAN'S STORY OF STROKE,
LOVE, AND SURVIVAL
A must read for stroke survivors and their families.
Bonnie Sherr Klein
$14.95 ISBN 1-885171-45-5

STILL FRIENDS: LIVING HAPPILY EVER AFTER...EVEN
IF YOUR MARRIAGE FALLS APART
True stories of couples who have managed to keep their
friendships intact after splitting up.
Barbara Quick
$12.95 ISBN 1-885171-36-6

CALLING TEXAS HOME: A LIVELY LOOK AT WHAT IT
MEANS TO BE A TEXAN
Bursting with fascinating trivia, first-person accounts of
frontier days, curiosities, and legends of the people of
Texas.
Wells Teague
$14.95 ISBN 1-885171-38-4

CALLING CALIFORNIA HOME: A LIVELY LOOK AT
WHAT IT MEANS TO BE A CALIFORNIAN
A cornucopia of facts and trivia about Californians and
the California Spirit.
Heather Waite
$14.95 ISBN 1-885171-37-4

CALLING THE MIDWEST HOME: A LIVELY LOOK AT
THE ORIGINS, ATTITUDES, QUIRKS, AND CURIOSITIES
OF AMERICA'S HEARTLANDERS
A loving look at the people who call the Midwest
home—whether they live there or not.
Carolyn Lieberg
$14.95 ISBN 1-885171-12-9

BREASTS: OUR MOST PUBLIC PRIVATE PARTS
One hundred and one women reveal the naked truth
about breasts.
Meema Spadola
$13.95 ISBN 1-885171-27-7

I WAS MY MOTHER'S BRIDESMAID: YOUNG ADULTS
TALK ABOUT THRIVING IN A BLENDED FAMILY
The truth about growing up in a "combined family."
Erica Carlisle and Vanessa Carlisle
$13.95 ISBN 1-885171-34-X

THE COURAGE TO BE A STEPMOM: FINDING YOUR
PLACE WITHOUT LOSING YOURSELF
Hands-on advice and emotional support for stepmothers.
Sue Patton Thoele
$14.95 ISBN 1-885171-28-5

CELEBRATING FAMILY: OUR LIFELONG BONDS WITH
PARENTS AND SIBLINGS
True stories about how baby boomers have recognized the
flaws of their families and come to love them as they are.
Lisa Braver Moss
$13.95 ISBN 1-885171-30-7

Aunties: Our Older, Cooler, Wiser Friends
An affectionate tribute to the unique and wonderful
women we call "Auntie."
Tamara Traeder and Julienne Bennett
$12.95 ISBN 1-885171-22-6

The Aunties Keepsake Book: The Story of Our
Friendship
A beautiful way to tell the wonderful story of you and
your auntie or niece.
Tamara Traeder and Julienne Bennett
$19.95 ISBN 1-885171-29-3

Little Sisters: The Last But Not The Least
A feisty look at the trials and tribulations, joys and
advantages of being a little sister.
Carolyn Lieberg
$13.95 ISBN 1-885171-24-2

girlfriends: Invisible Bonds, Enduring Ties
Filled with true stories of ordinary women and extraordi-
nary friendships.
Carmen Renee Berry and Tamara Traeder
$12.95 ISBN 1-885171-08-0
Also Available: Hardcover gift edition, $20.00
ISBN 1-885171-20-X

girlfriends TALK ABOUT MEN: SHARING SECRETS FOR A
GREAT RELATIONSHIP
This book shares insights from real women in real rela-
tionships—not just from the "experts."
Carmen Renee Berry and Tamara Traeder
$14.95 ISBN 1-885171-21-8

girlfriends FOR LIFE: FRIENDSHIPS WORTH KEEPING
FOREVER
This follow-up to the best-selling girlfriends is an all-new
collection of stories and anecdotes about the amazing
bonds of women's friendships.
Carmen Renee Berry and Tamara Traeder
$13.95 ISBN 1-885171-32-3

A girlfriends GIFT: REFLECTIONS ON THE
EXTRAORDINARY BONDS OF FRIENDSHIP
A lively collection of hundreds of quotations from the
girlfriends books series.
Carmen Renee Berry and Tamara Traeder
$15.95 ISBN 1-885171-43-9

A Couple of Friends: The Remarkable Friendship
between Straight Women and Gay Men
What makes the friendships between straight women
and gay men so wonderful? Find out in this honest and
fascinating book.
Robert H. Hopcke and Laura Rafaty
$14.95 ISBN 1-885171-33-1

Independent Women: Creating Our Lives, Living
Our Visions
How women value independence and relationship and
are redefining their lives to accommodate both.
Debra Sands Miller
$16.95 ISBN 1-885171-25-0

Those Who Can...Coach! Celebrating Coaches
Who Make a Difference
Inspirational stories from men and women who remem-
ber a coach who made a lasting difference in their lives.
Lorraine Glennon and Roy Leavitt
$12.95 ISBN 1-885171-49-8

Those Who Can...Teach! Celebrating Teachers
Who Make a Difference
A tribute to our nation's teachers.
Lorraine Glennon and Mary Mohler
$12.95 ISBN 1-885171-35-8

LIVING WITH DOGS: TALES OF LOVE, COMMITMENT &
ENDURING FRIENDSHIP
A tribute to our unique friendship with dogs—a great
gift for any "dog person."
Henry and Mary Ellen Korman
$13.95 ISBN 1-885171-19-6

THE WORRYWART'S COMPANION: TWENTY-ONE WAYS
TO SOOTHE YOURSELF AND WORRY SMART
The perfect gift for anyone who lies awake at night
worrying.
Dr. Beverly Potter
$11.95 ISBN 1-885171-15-3

DIAMONDS OF THE NIGHT: THE SEARCH FOR SPIRIT IN
YOUR DREAMS
Combines the story of "Annie" with a therapist's wisdom
about the power of dreams.
James Hagan, Ph.D.
$16.95 ISBN 1-879290-12-X

Books are available at fine retailers nationwide.

Prices subject to change without notice.

SOUTHEASTERN COMMUNITY COLLEGE LIBRARY

3 3255 00072 3388

SOUTHEASTERN COMMUNITY
COLLEGE LIBRARY
WHITEVILLE, NC 28472